The Rise and Fall of the Roman Empire

Johnathan Hamilton

Copyright © [2023]

Author: Johnathan Hamilton

Title: The Rise and Fall of the Roman Empire

All rights reserved. No part of this book may be reproduced or transmitted in any form or by any means, electronic or mechanical, including photocopying, recording, or by any information storage and retrieval system, without permission in writing from the author.

This book is a product of

ISBN:

Table of content

Chapter name	Page No
1. the transition from the Roman Republic to the Roman Empire	1
2. Imperial Growth and a Period of Great Success	16
3. Difficulties & Problems"	31
4. Western Roman Empire's Decline"	45
5. The Continuation of the Roman Empire in the East"	59
6. Influence and lasting impact"	74
7. Important People in Roman History	89
8. The Roman Way of Life	105
9. Roman Military Technology	121
10. Historical Analysis and Contexts	136

Chapter 1:
the transition from the Roman Republic to the Roman Empire

1.1. Introduction to the Roman Republic

An Amazing Trip Through Time, The Roman Republic

The Roman Republic was an incredibly significant and long-lasting political institution. Its influence on the evolution of government, law, and culture across the globe has been profound. An intriguing tale of aspiration, struggle, and development, this experiment in self-governance dates back over two and a half millennia. As we explore the history of the Roman Republic, we will learn more about its establishment, administration, and final fall.

Creating the Roman Republic, Part I

In the early sixth century BC, the Roman Republic arose in the centre of Italy's bountiful fields as a response to the Roman people's rising demand for political representation and independence. Its formation can be traced to more pragmatic circumstances, notwithstanding the fabled founding account of Romulus and Remus, twin brothers fostered by a she-wolf. From the wealthy patricians to the poor plebeians, Rome was a city where the struggle for power and influence was always just below the surface.

The Roman Republic was founded in 509 BC after the Roman people, led by Lucius Junius Brutus, destroyed the Etruscan monarchy. This was a watershed moment in Roman history, as the country changed from a monarchy to a republic with a system of checks and balances designed to prevent any one group or individual from gaining total power.

The Roman Republic's Institutions, Part II

The Roman Republic was distinguished by its complex structure of government. There were several different institutions in the republic, all of which had important purposes.

Roman republican government revolved around the Senate. It was a group of wise men, mostly drawn from the ranks of the Roman patrician class. By advising magistrates, formulating policies, and approving or rejecting legislation, the Senate had tremendous sway over Roman politics.

The Magistrates were elected people in charge of carrying out the law and running Rome's government. Different magistrates had different roles, such as the consuls, praetors, and aediles.

Third, there was the Assembly, which was made up of Roman citizens and was vested with the authority to establish laws, choose magistrates, and settle major issues. Different groups within the population were represented in their own assemblies, such as the Centuriate Assembly and the Tribal Assembly.

For their part, the plebeians chose a group of representatives known as the Tribunes, who had the power to veto any decision made by the judges or the Senate that they felt went against the interests of the common people.

Censors were Roman officials in charge of maintaining order and collecting a census of the population. When it came to matters of public morality and social standing, they wielded substantial influence.

To prevent any one person or group from amassing unlimited power, these organisations woven a complicated web of governance. The stability of the Roman Republic can be traced back to this system of checks and balances.

The Third: Growth and Military Might

Growth in territory was a defining element of the Roman Republic's history. It was once an Italian city-state, but it grew fast through conquest. The military might and discipline of Rome were crucial factors in this development.

The Roman legions were a powerful army because of their training and discipline. They played a crucial role in the subjugation of regional rivals and the spread of the republic's dominance across the Mediterranean. Rome's empire grew as a result of notable conflicts like the Punic Wars against Carthage and the exploits of Julius Caesar.

Issues Associated with Growth

Expansion into new territories offered Rome riches and power, but also presented new obstacles. The wealthy elite amassed great fortunes while the masses suffered as a result of the wealth explosion. The ability of the Roman republic to govern was also put to the test by the conquest of new areas, which brought with them a wide variety of peoples and civilizations.

Tiberius and Gaius Gracchi, two brothers, were among the first to speak out about these problems. With the hope of reducing social tensions, they pushed for land reform and the allocation of land to the landless poor. They were killed because of the opposition they faced from the conservative senatorial elite, and their killings set a precedent for the violent political confrontations that would characterise the last years of the republic.

The Decline and Fall of the Roman Republic

Many things contributed to the fall of the Roman Republic, but two major turning points were the ascent of powerful military generals and the weakening of democratic standards.

Generals rose to prominence as a result of Rome's military victories, winning the respect and allegiance of the army as a result. This allegiance was used by leaders like Marius, Sulla, and Caesar to undermine the Senate's authority. The conflict between Marius and Sulla, which eventually led to Sulla's tyranny, was the first major departure from republican principles.

This power battle accelerated the deterioration of the political standards that had regulated Roman politics for generations. Crime, corruption, and the threat or use of force in politics all became routine. Disregard for established republican procedures was epitomised by the First Triumvirate of Caesar, Pompey, and Crassus.

The final nail in the coffin of the republic was driven in 44 BC, when, after defeating Pompey and the Senate, Julius Caesar proclaimed himself dictator for life. The stability of the republic was not fully restored after his death on the Ides of March in 44 BC. The ensuing power vacuum sparked a string of civil wars, ultimately ending with Octavian (later known as Augustus) as the victor. As the first Roman Emperor, his reign began in 27 BC and marked the end of the Roman Republic.

Roman Civilization's Lasting Impact

The influence of the Roman Republic has lasted for centuries. Its government model, with its emphasis on checks and balances, was influential in the development of many contemporary democracies. The foundation for modern legal systems in the West was established by the just and equitable Roman law system. The Romans' influence on European language development can be seen even in the legacy of their Latin language.

The Roman Republic has always fascinated people because of the intricate web of ambition, struggle, and reinvention that shaped its history and political institutions. It's a sobering reminder of what might happen when political factions clash and republican institutions crack.

The story of the Roman Republic's development from a small city-state to a massive empire is fascinating. Its institutions, struggles, and final death continue to fascinate academics and enthusiasts alike because they teach us so much about the nuances of human ambition, power dynamics, and government. The Roman Republic is a symbol of Rome's enduring legacy and the significant impact it had on the development of Western civilisation.

1.2. Transformation into the Roman Empire under Augustus

The Rise of the Roman Empire and the End of the Roman Republic

The rise of Augustus to power and the subsequent transformation of the Roman Republic into the Roman Empire was a watershed moment in the development of the ancient Roman state. This shift remade the Mediterranean world's political, social, and cultural landscape, paving the way for centuries of imperial domination. Here, we'll investigate the many interconnected causes that brought about the establishment of the Roman Empire and Augustus's rule.

Part I: The Fall of the Roman Empire

The Roman Republic was in a state of growing instability by the end of the first century BCE. The republican institutions and values that had governed Rome for centuries had been weakened by political corruption, economic inequity, and a succession of civil wars. The republic was weak and fragmented because to power battles between important generals like Marius, Sulla, Pompey, and Julius Caesar.

Rome was thrown into disarray with the assassination of Julius Caesar in 44 BCE, with his supporters led by Mark Antony and his assassins by conspirators Brutus and Cassius. Octavian (later known as Augustus) beat Mark Antony and Cleopatra in the decisive Battle of Actium in 31 BCE, so becoming the only ruler of Rome.

Part Two: Augustus' Ascendancy

Augustus, or Gaius Octavius, was Caesar's adopted grandson and nephew. After Caesar's death, he became a major player in the subsequent power struggle. After Augustus' triumph at Actium, he concluded that the old republican government was doomed. He undertook radical reforms to restore order and strengthen his grip on power.

Augustus was careful not to accept the title of dictator or king when he established the Principate, as doing so would have been considered as a betrayal of republican values. He instead proclaimed himself the "First Citizen" (Princeps) and instituted the Principate, a new form of government that kept some republican traditions but centralised authority in his hands.

Augustus began a time of social and economic reforms, which allowed for the subsequent period of reconstruction. To reestablish order in Roman society, he tried to reconstruct the city of Rome, invest in its infrastructure, and advocate for the moral and cultural ideals he considered essential.

Third, Augustus ended the Republic's decades of civil conflict with the Pax Romana. During his rule, Rome's frontiers were secure, trade prospered, and the empire experienced a time of prosperity known as the Pax Romana.

The Changing Roman Empire, Part III

The political and administrative structure of Rome changed drastically under Augustus. Once the most influential political body, the Roman Senate is now mostly advisory. By retaining a number of republican offices, Augustus preserved the facade of a republican government while consolidating power in his own hands.

Augustus's multiple titles and posts centralised power in his person, making him the Emperor. He held multiple titles, including "princeps," "imperator," and "pontifex maximus." His ability to appoint and remove generals and legions from their positions was a particularly significant aspect of his authority over the military.

The Augustan Principate: Augustus meticulously crafted a public persona that reflected the best of ancient Roman values. He advocated virtuous behaviour and respect for Roman customs as a means of ensuring the survival of the state. The goal of this philosophical revolution was to revitalise national pride and solidarity.

Third, Augustus instituted administrative reforms that led to a more streamlined way of running the Roman provinces. He formed a permanent professional force called the Praetorian Guard to keep the peace in Rome. The foundation for the future prosperity of the Roman Empire was established by his administrative reforms.

Augustan Age Cultural Prosperity

Augustus was a supporter of the arts and literature in addition to his political leadership. The Augustan Age, which flourished during his rule, left an unmistakable influence on Roman art and architecture.

Augustus promoted and admired literary figures like Virgil, Horace, and Ovid, whose works lauded Roman culture and the emperor's accomplishments. The "Aeneid," an epic poem by Virgil, is widely considered a classic of Roman literature and mythology.

Augustus also made important contributions to the city of Rome's built environment by constructing new public buildings and restoring ancient temples. The Ara Pacis, a monumental altar to the Roman goddess of peace, is among the most well-known structures from the Augustan period.

Imperial Rome and the Aftermath of Augustus

The expansion of Rome under Augustus and his policies changed the course of history. The Principate he established paved the way for the long-lasting Roman Empire.

First, the Roman Empire was made stable and durable by Augustus's meticulous consolidation of power and administrative reforms. The Roman Empire flourished under his successors, growing in size and power to encompass lands as far apart as Britain and Egypt.

Augustus established a norm by making the emperor a deity, ushering in a long-standing custom known as the Imperial Cult. It was through this religious adulation that the Emperor's power was maintained.

The Roman Empire left an enduring legacy in the areas of law, language, architecture, and governance, all of which are still felt today. The Romance languages are descended from Latin, and many modern legal systems are based on Roman law.

In conclusion, Augustus' leadership over Rome's transition from republic to empire was a watershed moment in the annals of humankind. The foundation for centuries of imperial control was laid during Augustus's reign, which brought stability, prosperity, and cultural blossoming to Rome. His influence as a political leader and artistic patron lives on, reminding us of Rome's profound effect on the development of Western civilisation. The Roman Empire, which emerged from this transition, would forever alter the global political landscape.

1.3. Key figures and events during the early empire

Major People and Events in the Rise of the Roman Empire

Following the founding of the Roman Empire under the authority of Augustus, the early Roman Empire, also known as the Principate, was a time of tremendous transition and consolidation of power. Key personalities rose to prominence during this time, and they would go on to play essential roles in directing the course of the Roman Empire. Our investigation will focus on the major players and events that shaped the foundation of the Roman Empire.

Augustus I (reigned 27 BC-14 AD)

Augustus, or Gaius Octavius, was a pivotal player in the rise of the Roman Empire. From the anarchy of the waning Roman Republic, where he stood as Caesar's adoptive son and heir, he emerged victorious. By gaining authority while keeping up the appearance of republican rule, Augustus deftly navigated the perilous seas of Roman politics.

Augustus became the first Roman Emperor, but he was cautious to keep the republican trappings of power intact. He was both princeps (first citizen) and imperator (commander), giving him absolute power under the guise of a republican government.

Augustus made more effective administrative reforms, including the reorganisation of the Roman provinces, the creation of a professional standing army, and the standardisation of paperwork. His reforms ensured the Roman Empire's continuity and set the stage for its continued prosperity.

The Pax Romana was a time of relative peace and prosperity in the Roman Empire that began during Augustus's reign. There was peace and prosperity across the empire at this time.

A.D. 14–37 II. Tiberius

Tiberius became the second Roman Emperor after Augustus. The reign of his family, the Julio-Claudians, bridged the gap between the founding figure of Augustus and the succession of emperors.

First, Tiberius had the unenviable burden of following in the footsteps of the legendary Augustus. During his rule, he worked hard to solidify his position as ruler and keep the empire secure.

Tiberius furthered the imperial government's consolidation of power. To guarantee his own safety and maintain his authority, he increased the Praetorian Guard's responsibilities as the emperor's personal bodyguard.

Tiberius' decline as he aged brought terror and political intrigue to Rome as he became more secluded and suspicious. After his death, his successor, Caligula, would take over a difficult empire.

Caligula III (AD 37-41)

One of the more infamous figures in Roman history was Caligula, whose given name was Gaius. His chaotic and short rule was defined by lavish spending, brutality, and scandal.

One, Caligula rose to prominence quickly after assuming power, and he was initially well-received by the populace. However, he quickly began exhibiting worrisome behaviour. He acted in a flamboyant and peculiar manner, proclaiming himself a god and building a pontoon bridge across the Bay of Baiae, for example.

The Senate and the Praetorian Guard resisted Caligula's tyranny because of his cruelty and paranoia. His popularity plummeted as a result of his executions and banishment of people he deemed to be threats.

The assassination of Caligula by the Praetorian Guard in the year 41 A.D. brought an end to his reign. A lesson about the perils of unchecked imperial power and the potential for tyranny can be learned from his tenure.

Claudius IV (reigned AD 41-54)

After Caligula's death, his uncle Claudius suddenly ascended to the throne of Rome. During his rule, things finally began to settle down and get run more smoothly.

After the chaos of Caligula's rule, Claudius' first priority was to establish a sense of order and stability. He began building aqueducts and roadways, among other infrastructure projects.

Second, the empire became larger under Claudius' watch as he directed the invasion and eventual incorporation of Britain. Rome gained a lot of territory as a result of this expansion.

Third, Claudius undertook a number of legal reforms, one of which was to award Roman citizenship to the citizens of certain regions. Under his leadership, Roman law advanced further.

Nero, Virgilio (54–68 AD)

The last of the Julio-Claudian emperors, Nero, is remembered today for his lavish spending, cruelty, and the destruction of Rome in the Great Fire.

1. Quick Rise to Power: Nero took the throne at a young age and was initially supported by wise counsellors. His authority, however, took a sinister turn as he grew older.

An enormous fire ripped through Rome in the year 64 AD, causing widespread devastation. The Emperor Nero's reputation was damaged by his response, which included false rumours that he had played the lyre as Rome burnt.

Thirdly, Nero is remembered for starting Rome's first persecution of Christians. Christians were held responsible for the blaze and brutally persecuted as a result.

Nero's rule ended in uprising and public upheaval, which led to his own suicide. In 68 A.D., with a revolt looming, he took his own life, effectively ending the reign of the Julio-Claudian dynasty.

Sixth Century A.D., or the Year of the Four Emperors.

There was rapid succession and civil war in Roman history during the Year of the Four Emperors.

First, there was Galba, a seasoned general who became emperor after Nero's death. His collapse was a result of his severe policies and his inability to win over the Praetorian Guard.

2. Otho: Otho, a previous governor, deposed Galba but was himself challenged by other pretenders to the throne.

Thirdly, Vitellius, governor of an adjacent province, rose to prominence as a potential heir to the throne and briefly held the title of emperor.

4. Vespasian: Vespasian, a capable general, triumphed in the end of this bloody conflict. Under his leadership, the Flavian dynasty was established, and peace and order were restored to Rome.

Emperor Vespasian's (Reign: 69–79 AD)

After the chaos of the Year of the Four Emperors, military leader Vespasian restored order to the Roman Empire.

To help replenish the empire's coffers following the civil wars, Vespasian enacted substantial financial reforms, one of which was a levy on public urinals in Rome (the "urine tax").

Construction Projects: He began work on what would become one of Rome's most recognisable landmarks, the Flavian Amphitheatre (or Colosseum).

Third, the Jewish War continued under Vespasian's reign and was finally won by his son Titus when he captured Jerusalem in 70 AD.

The Eighth Dynasty: The Flavian

Vespasian, Titus, and Domitian ruled under the Flavian dynasty, which brought peace and prosperity to the Roman Empire after the upheaval of the late Julio-Claudian period.

During his brief reign, Titus (son of Vespasian) oversaw the construction of the Colosseum and the aftermath of the devastating eruption of Mount Vesuvius (79 AD).

 put under ground; buried Pompeii.

Second, Domitian (reign 81–96 AD), younger brother of Titus, was a capable administrator who grew increasingly dictatorial and paranoid. He set off an era of persecution against thinkers and believers in particular, such as Christians and philosophers.

IX. Summary

The early Roman Empire was a time of great change, with many emperors coming and going, each of them left their mark on the empire. Other emperors, such as Caligula and Nero, left a legacy of tyranny and excess, while others, such as Augustus and Claudius, contributed to the stability and prosperity of the empire. Succession struggles, civil conflicts, and the intricate interplay of politics and power characterised this pivotal age.

The foundation was laid by the early Roman Empire for what would become one of the longest-lasting and most significant civilizations in human history. As it expanded its frontiers and encountered new cultures and peoples in the centuries to ahead, it would inevitably change and face new obstacles. Insights into the intricacies of leadership and government, as well as the Roman Empire's continuing impact on the world, can be gleaned from the legacies of these early empire personalities and events, which remain a fascinating and essential chapter in the annals of human history.

Chapter 2:
" Imperial Growth and a Period of Great Success "

2.1. Rome's territorial expansion and conquests

Expanding and Conquering Rome's Neighbouring Lands

One of history's most recognisable civilizations, ancient Rome's territorial expansion and conquests are a testament to the ambition, military power, and organisational competence of its leaders. The Roman Republic and its successor, the Roman Empire, ruled over a large territory that spanned three continents over the period of several centuries. This extraordinary expedition of conquest and colonisation changed the face of ancient geopolitics and left a legacy that is still felt today across the globe. We shall examine the significant events, policies, and outcomes of Rome's territorial expansion.

The Italian Peninsula and the Beginnings of Expansion I.

The history of Rome's expansion may be traced back to its earliest attempts to assert dominance across the Italian Peninsula. Rome was one of many Italian city-states in antiquity, and it rose to prominence through a complicated web of alliances and conflicts.

In the early years of the Roman Republic, Rome became a member of the Latin League, a confederation of cities that shared a common language, Latin. The Romans gained crucial military experience from this partnership, and they were able to more easily establish their rule over central Italy as a result.

Wars fought between the Romans and a confederation of Italic tribes known as the Samnites during Rome's conquest of southern Italy. The Roman military was put to the test and their rule of the territory was cemented throughout the course of three separate Samnite Wars (343-341 BC, 327-304 BC, and 298-290 BC).

Third, Rome's expanding sway in Italy drew the ire of King Pyrrhus of Epirus, Greece, sparking the Pyrrhic War. There were several bloody engagements during the Pyrrhic War (280-275 BC), which ultimately led to Pyrrhus's defeat and departure. Although Rome paid a high price in lives, their resiliency was on display in their wins.

Roman Confederation (4): Rome had a structure called as the Roman Confederation to oversee its expanding empire. This permitted conquered peoples to keep some of their independence while also allying with Rome and providing soldiers and resources.

Western Mediterranean Conquest (Part II): The Punic Wars

The Punic Wars were a string of battles between Rome and Carthage, a formidable North African empire. The victor of these conflicts would control the western Mediterranean.

The First Punic War (264-241 BC) was fought mostly at sea, and Rome responded by constructing a powerful navy to threaten Carthage's position as the preeminent naval power. Rome conquered Sicily, Sardinia, and Corsica after a long war and eventually came out on top.

The Second Punic War (218-201 BC) is famous for the daring invasion of Italy by the renowned Carthaginian general Hannibal. Hannibal was ultimately defeated by Roman general Scipio Africanus at the Battle of Zama, despite inflicting severe losses on the Romans. This victory was crucial in securing Spain and other lands for Rome.

Third Punic War (149-146 BC): Rome besieged Carthage as an act of final retribution and destroyed the city. As a result, Rome was able to exert even more influence over North Africa, effectively spelling the end of the Carthaginian Empire.

The Hellenistic East: Part III

Rome's territorial expansion also brought it into contact with the Hellenistic kingdoms that had been created by Alexander the Great's successors in the eastern Mediterranean.

First, during the Macedonian Wars (214-148 BC), Rome engaged in its first major confrontation with the Hellenistic civilization. Rome came out on top, expanding her empire by absorbing Macedonia and Greece.

Conflict with the Seleucid Empire arose as a result of Rome's advance into the eastern Mediterranean. Seleucid territory in Asia Minor were annexed by the Romans after their victory in the Syrian Wars (192-188 BC).

Third, Pergamon's 133 BC bequest to Rome of its territory greatly enlarged the Roman Empire's grip on Asia Minor.

The Invasion of Britain and France

The conquest of Gaul (modern-day France) by Julius Caesar, a general and statesman who would become a pivotal player in the decline of the Roman Republic and the ascent of the Roman Empire, is one of the most well-known episodes in Rome's territorial expansion.

First, Caesar's campaigns in Gaul (58-50 BC) solidified Roman rule over the area and made him a popular and influential figure in Rome. The campaigns are described in great detail in his Commentarii de Bello Gallico (Commentaries on the Gallic War).

The Roman invasion of Gaul and the subsequent introduction of Roman culture, law, and administration to the conquered territory resulted in the Romanization of Gaul.

Caesar also led two expeditions to Britannia (Britain) in 55 and 54 BC, but the Romans were unable to establish full control of the island at that time.

Conquest of Dacia, Part V

During Emperor Trajan's reign, the Roman Empire made considerable territorial gains in the Danube region with the invasion of Dacia (present-day Romania).

Emperor Trajan waged two campaigns (in 101–102 and 105–106 CE) against Dacian king Decebalus. By conquering Dacia, the Roman Empire gained access to its rich resources and new territory.

Trajan commissioned the erection of Trajan's Column in Rome to honour his victory. A spiral frieze representing events from the Dacian Wars wraps around the base of this structure.

Parthia and the Eastern Frontier in Chapter VI

Conflicts and territorial shifts ensued when the expanding Roman Empire came into contact with the Parthian Empire (in what is now Iran and Iraq).

First, the Parthian Campaigns: Conflicts with the Parthians characterised Roman military operations in the East, particularly those of Crassus and Antony. Although these operations accomplished little, some territory near the eastern border was realigned as a result.

To designate the boundary between the Roman and Parthian Empires, a number of client kingdoms and buffer states were established. For generations to come, this area would be fraught with danger and warfare.

What Happened After the Third Century Crisis

During the early years of the Principate, the Roman Empire's territorial expansion reached its pinnacle. The immense expanse of the empire, along with internal and foreign factors, led to its downfall and final disintegration.

The Roman Empire experienced internal strife, foreign invasions, economic uncertainty, and competing dynasties during the third century, known as the "Crisis of the Third Century" (AD 235-284). There were several different emperors running different parts of the empire at this time.

Second, the decline and fall: Western provinces of the Roman Empire fell victim to barbarian invasions, and this trend persisted as the empire shrank. The chasm between the Byzantine Empire in the east and the Western Roman Empire in the west widened.

Third, the Farthest Outpost: The limits of the Roman Empire shifted as it adapted to new external challenges like the Vandals, the Goths, and the Sassanids in Persia.

 Huns. The eventual collapse of the Western Roman Empire in 476 AD was hastened by the loss of crucial regions like North Africa and the Western Roman provinces.

Final Thoughts

The centuries-long and worldwide impact of Rome's territorial expansion and conquests cannot be overstated. Its administrative efficiency, military prowess, and cultural impact were all felt throughout the areas it conquered. The influence of Roman culture can be seen even today in the world's languages, buildings, and legal and political systems.

While internal strife and external pressures eventually brought down the Roman Empire, its growth and consolidation of territory stand as a testament to the ever-present human desire for power, prosperity, and influence. Lessons on the complexity of empire-building and the rise and fall of civilizations can be gleaned from the chronicle of Rome's territorial expansion, which provides a riveting narrative of ambition, struggle, and transition.

2.2. Pax Romana: Peace and prosperity

Peace and prosperity across the Roman Empire; the Pax Romana.

The "Roman Peace," or Pax Romana, was an era that has had a profound impact on the world. During these roughly 200 years, from 27 BC to 180 AD, the huge Roman Empire enjoyed unprecedented levels of peace, stability, and prosperity. A moment of exceptional prosperity, cultural flowering, and political stability for the Roman Empire. The Pax Romana was an era that made an unmistakable effect on the world, and we will examine its primary features, accomplishments, and legacies in this article.

I. The Seeds of Roman Peace

Augustus (sometimes spelt Octavian), the first Roman Emperor, established the basis for Roman peace and stability in 27 BC. By instituting a new form of government, Augustus ended the chaotic years of the Roman Republic and laid the groundwork for the Pax Romana.

First, Augustus instituted a number of important changes to keep the empire's interior in order and its borders safe. A professional standing army was formed, an effective taxation system was implemented, and Roman moral ideals were popularised as part of these changes.

When establishing the Principate, Augustus struck a delicate balance between the appearance of republican rule and the actuality of autocratic control. While he did diminish the Senate's authority, he nonetheless styled himself as "First Citizen" (Princeps) rather than a dictator or king, and the institution survived under his rule.

Augustus' military victories and conquests, including Egypt's absorption into the Roman Empire, boosted the empire's economy and population. This wealth was subsequently invested in public programmes and utilised to maintain peace and order.

Augustus and His Successors in the Roman Empire

The Pax Romana was initiated by Rome's first emperor, but it was maintained and expanded upon by his successors.

Trade and commerce within the empire flourished as a result of Augustus and succeeding emperors' investments in infrastructure projects like roads, aqueducts, and ports, leading to economic growth. During this time, the Roman economy flourished like never before.

Second, there was a cultural rebirth during the Pax Romana. Roman literature was shaped by the likes of Virgil, Horace, and Ovid, while the visual arts, architecture, and sculpture of the time reached new heights.

Third, domestic peace and prosperity resulted from the Pax Romana, which made it possible for Rome's cities to flourish as major economic, cultural, and political hubs. The Colosseum and the Pantheon in Rome were both built during this time period and are now considered symbols of that era.

The Spread of Roman Authority, Part III

Not only did the Roman Empire expand its frontiers during the Pax Romana, but it also enjoyed a time of relative stability within those confines.
The Roman Empire was expanded to include the island of Great Britain after a victorious invasion led by Emperor Claudius I in 43 A.D.

To further solidify the Pax Romana, the Romans annexed the territories of Thrace (today's Bulgaria and parts of Greece) and Mauretania (today's Algeria and Morocco).

Third, Rome built a system of client kingdoms and alliances that allowed it to exert power well beyond its borders, bringing numerous neighbouring countries under Roman protection and allowing them to participate in Roman trade.

Roman Law and Governmental Structures

Modern legal and administrative frameworks can be traced back to the foundations provided by Roman law and governance during the Pax Romana.

The "Twelve Tables" and the work of jurists like Gaius and Ulpian, among others, represent the culmination of the Pax Romana's influence on Roman law. Justice, fairness, and the safeguarding of personal liberties were central tenets of Roman law.

Second, the Roman Empire's administration was remarkably effective, allowing for widespread taxation, road upkeep, and the fair dispensation of law and order.

While Rome maintained central power, it often let local districts to govern themselves in accordance with their customs and traditions during the Pax Romana period. The stability of the empire was bolstered by this adaptability.

Conflicts and difficulties

Despite its reputation for tranquilly, the Pax Romana was not without of difficulties and wars.
Various barbarian groups, such as the Germanic tribes to the north and the Parthians to the east, posed challenges to the Roman Empire

from the outside. Diplomacy and military efforts helped to contain these dangers, but constant attention was still necessary.

The Roman Empire was so large that it even caused internal tensions to occasionally boil over. Instability in government and attempts to kill rulers also occurred.

Third Century Crisis: Multiple king claims, economic troubles, and invasions marked this time of turbulence, which emerged towards the end of the Pax Romana. The Roman Empire's decline started at this point.

Pax Romana: Sixth Century Aftermath

The Pax Romana left behind an enduring legacy that is still felt today.First, the concept of individual rights and justice, as well as the structure of modern legal systems, owe a great deal to Roman law and governing principles.Latin, the language of Rome, inspired the growth of Western literature, philosophy, and science, and its heritage lives on in the Romance languages.

The Pax Romana's engineering feats, including as its roads, aqueducts, and buildings, are still studied and respected today.

Throughout history, political philosophers and politicians have looked to the concept of a stable and orderly government as a model for how to handle massive geographical expansion.
Final ThoughtsThe Pax Romana was an extraordinary time in human history, proof that a civilisation could reach previously unimaginable heights of stability and cultural development. It's a symbol of how long people have been trying to find peace and prosperity. Even though the Roman Empire fell victim to both internal and foreign factors, the Pax Romana left an indelible mark on the way we think about government, the rule of law, and the potential for a harmonious and wealthy society.

2.3. Cultural achievements and innovations

What Ancient Rome Contributed Culturally and How It Changed the World

The cultural contributions and innovations of ancient Rome have had a profound impact on the development of civilization. The contributions of ancient Rome, one of the world's most powerful civilizations, may be seen in subjects as diverse as literature, art, architecture, and engineering. This study dives into the diverse fabric of Roman civilization, illuminating landmark developments that have lasting relevance today.

The First: Words and Stories

One of the greatest legacies of Roman culture is the Latin language, which is still widely spoken today. It laid the groundwork for the Romance languages and continues to inform the development of legal, scientific, and medical jargon in those languages.

2 Classical writing The Romans, steeped in Greek culture, created a wealth of writing that has stood the test of time. Among the most famous Roman authors is Virgil, whose epic poem "The Aeneid" is fundamental to Roman history, culture, and identity. Horace, Ovid, and Livy are also important characters because their historical writings shed light on Roman society and culture.

Oratory and public speaking have been greatly influenced by Cicero, a true master of rhetoric and oratory. His intellectual writings, correspondence, and speeches are still studied because of their eloquence and relevance today.

The Built Environment and Engineering
The Romans were forerunners in many aspects of architecture, including the construction of arches and domes. Buildings like the

Pantheon attest to the Romans' engineering brilliance. The semicircular shape of the Roman arch became an integral part of architecture and continues to have an impact on contemporary styles.

Second, aqueducts: Roman engineers built a complex network of aqueducts to bring water from faraway springs to populated areas. The water supply of Rome was secured by these engineering feats, which also served as a model for water management in subsequent civilizations.

The Roman road network, known for its durability and efficiency, linked the remote corners of the empire together, and the Roman bridges were as impressive. The Pont du Gard in France, built with Roman concrete, is one of the world's longest-lasting bridges.

The Colosseum is one of the most recognisable monuments of ancient Rome and a tribute to Roman engineering and architectural excellence. This enormous amphitheatre hosted gladiator fights and other public spectacles for an audience of up to 80,000 people.

The Fine Arts, Part 3

One, Roman art and sculpture demonstrated a dedication to realism and portraiture. The likenesses of famous people, such as emperors and heads of state, were captured in sculptures and busts with remarkable accuracy.

Roman homes and public buildings alike featured beautiful mosaics on the floors and walls. These intricate paintings showed stories from mythology, everyday life, and historical events.

Frescoes were a popular form of Roman decoration, and they provided a window into the era's aesthetic and cultural preferences.

The frescoes of Pompeii and Herculaneum are particularly well-known because they were saved by the eruption of Mount Vesuvius.

Law and Administration

Rule of law, fairness, and protection of personal liberties were all important tenets of the Roman legal system. One of the earliest attempts to codify Roman law, the "Twelve Tables" laid the groundwork for contemporary legal systems.

The Roman Republic was an early example for effective government due to its elaborate system of checks and balances, which was administered by the Senate. The Senate, made up of elected individuals, served as a place for debate and policymaking that influenced the development of modern democracies.

The Roman Empire had well-oiled administrative machinery, what with its provinces, its professional civil service, and its elaborate tax collection infrastructure. These advancements in government policy made it possible for the empire to conquer vast swaths of land.

V. Urban Development and Physical Facilities

Roman cities often had public bathhouses (thermae) that served as both hygienic facilities and social hubs for residents to unwind and get to know one another. These showers were generally elaborate works of architecture and included heating systems.

Roman sewer systems, such as the Cloaca Maxima, were among the first of their kind, allowing for the effective management and treatment of wastewater in highly populated areas.

In addition to the Colosseum, public spaces such as amphitheatres, forums, and marketplaces were prominent features of Roman urban planning. These community centres were built in the style of classical Rome.

Syncretism and the Spread of Cultures

Roman culture developed through the adoption of elements from the cultures the Roman Empire conquered and ruled over. The complex tapestry of Roman culture was woven in part by the mixing of many religious beliefs, artistic styles, and culinary traditions brought about by syncretism.

Romanization was the process through which Roman culture, language, and practises were diffused across the vast Roman Empire. Under Roman authority, many different societies and locations benefited from this process of cultural amalgamation.

Influence and Legacies, Part VII

Ancient Rome's legacy of cultural contributions and technological advancements lives on in countless ways today.

Roman law provides a foundation for justice and the safeguarding of individual liberties in many modern legal systems.

Latin, the language of Rome, is still used widely in education and nomenclature, and ancient Roman literature is widely read and admired.

Thirdly, engineering and architecture: The arch and concrete are just two examples of how Roman innovations continue to influence today's building and infrastructure practises.

Roman republicanism, political philosophy, and administrative architecture have all had a lasting impact on modern political theory and practise.

The visual arts and aesthetics have been profoundly influenced by classical Roman painting, sculpture, and architecture.

The legacy of cultural syncretism and the flow of ideas continues to shape the diversity and understanding of cultures around the world.

In conclusion, ancient Rome's cultural contributions and innovations have left a significant and enduring legacy that continues to influence the world today. The Romans were one of the most influential ancient civilizations, and their contributions to the fields of language, law, architecture, and government are still felt today. The cultural achievements of ancient Rome will continue to serve as an example of the human capacity for innovation and change.

Chapter 3:
"Difficulties & Problems"

3.1. Economic and social challenges

Difficulties with Ancient Rome's Economy and Society

The Roman Empire experienced economic and social issues throughout its long and illustrious history, although these are sometimes overlooked in light of the city's famed splendour and might. A variety of economic and social concerns shaped Rome's rise and eventual downfall, despite the city's reputation for technological innovation, architectural marvels, and military power. The primary economic and social problems that afflicted Rome will be investigated, as will their effects on the empire over time.

I. Financial Difficulties

Revenue Collection and Taxation

Rome's need for money to run its massive empire was a major problem. Overtaxation was a common problem for Roman residents and provincials alike, even though taxes was essential for funding the military, infrastructure projects, and the bureaucracy.

Some affluent people and landowners find ways to avoid paying their fair share of taxes by engaging in dishonest behaviour or taking advantage of legal loopholes. Because of this, the government was forced to receive less money.

Provinces under heavy exploitation typically resisted Roman rule because of the heavy levy imposed on them. Costly tribute demands have the potential to destroy local economies.

Second, Economic Disparity:

Economic disparity was a problem in ancient Rome, as it was in many other civilizations. The affluent elite, known as patricians, controlled the majority of the country's wealth and resources, while the plebeians and slaves made up the rest of the population and had few economic options.

The redistribution of land and the availability of farmland were perennial issues. The elite resisted reforms to land ownership, such as the Gracchi brothers' planned Lex Agraria.

Rome's economy was dependent on slave labour, which led to the rise of a massive slave-owning aristocracy. Slavery exacerbated existing inequalities and fueled social discontent.

Depreciating currency:

Currency devaluation occurred periodically in the Roman economy due to overminting of coins, inflation, and the cost of running the empire.

Reduced precious metal content in Roman coins, known as "debasement," eroded trust in the currency and contributed to economic unsteadiness.

- Inflation: residents had trouble affording basic necessities as prices rose, a trend generally linked to the devaluation of currency.

Conquest's Financial Impact:

The necessity of acquiring additional lands and resources was a major factor in Rome's expansionist policies. The empire grew dependent on the ongoing conquest of new lands and the collection of tribute from those territories.

Constant growth put a burden on Roman supplies and the army, which in turn made expansion even more necessary. The benefits of the empire's conquests began to dwindle over time.

Social Difficulties, Part II

1) Slavery and the Class Structure:

The institution of slavery ran deep through Roman culture and significantly altered social relations. Slaves were a large part of the population and were used for everything from menial labour to academic instruction.

Differences in rights and opportunities arose as a result of Rome's strict social hierarchy, which placed citizens at the top, followed by non-citizen dwellers, and last, slaves. Unrest spread because of the dehumanising effects of slavery.

- Slave Rebellions: Throughout Roman history, there were multiple slave revolts, the most well-known of which occurred during the time of Spartacus in the first century BC. The strain and instability that slavery inevitably brings to a society were on full display during these uprisings.

Family breakdown in Roman society

Roman culture historically placed a premium on family life. However, the conventional family structure began to collapse as a result of social developments such as the dropping birthrate among the Roman aristocracy and the shift towards more independent lives.

Conflicts between the pursuit of material success and social status and more traditional family values have contributed to the weakening of family ties and shifting patterns of succession.

Population reduction and demographic changes are attributed in part to the declining birthrate among the Roman elite. The long-term workforce and military recruitment of the empire were both affected by this demographic transition.

Urbanisation and population growth:

Overcrowding, a lack of suitable housing, and a lack of reliable public services were all problems that arose as Rome expanded into a major urban centre. Large-scale societal shifts and difficulties emerged as a result of urbanisation.

The poor in cities often had to make do with substandard housing, which lacked basic amenities like running water and proper sanitation due to the housing crisis. Tenements and slums proliferated.

Overcrowding and lack of adequate sanitation helped spread diseases throughout metropolitan areas, impacting people of all socioeconomic backgrounds.

Decreased participation in civic life

Many Roman citizens lost interest in politics as the empire grew and authority was consolidated in Rome. Consequences for the Republic and later the Empire were felt as civic involvement and participation declined.

People were appeased and their attention was diverted from political difficulties by offering them free food (bread) and entertainment (circuses and gladiatorial games).

Many people relied on affluent benefactors for financial and social support, which weakened their ability to participate in society and provide for themselves.

The Final Words

Rome's complex and ever-evolving society was inextricably linked to the social and economic issues it encountered throughout its history. Although Rome was a cultural and political powerhouse, it struggled with difficulties of economic disparity, social stratification, and political instability even as it produced some truly amazing works of architecture and art. The decline and fall of the Roman Empire can be traced back in large part to these internal and foreign difficulties.

However, the lessons learnt from Rome's tribulations are just as important as the city's monumental triumphs in perpetuating the city's heritage. Learning about ancient Rome may teach us about the possibilities and limitations of the human mind, as well as the difficulties of leading large populations in complex civilizations. As modern societies face their own challenges and objectives, they can learn from Rome's history and the lessons it provides about the intricacies of politics, economics, and society.

3.2. Political instability and succession crises

Ancient Rome's Political Uncertainty and Succession Problems

Politics in ancient Rome were often unstable, and succession crises challenged the continuity of both the Roman Republic and the Roman Empire. Rome had a difficult time with power transfers, managing political groups, and settling conflicts between ambitious leaders, despite its continuing impact and accomplishments. The purpose of this investigation is to dive into the most important cases of political instability and succession crises in ancient Rome, analysing their origins, outcomes, and lasting lessons.

The Roman Republic's Balancing Act, Part I

First, the battle between the ranks:

This conflict between the patricians (the aristocratic elite) and the plebeians (the common people) was a major cause of instability in the early Roman Republic. Conflicts erupted and social and legal changes were demanded because the plebeians wanted more political power and representation.

The post of tribune was created so that the concerns of the common people could be heard and acted upon. Tribunes may veto Senate and other official actions, creating some checks and balances in the government.

Military leaders' influence and clout:

Military leaders and generals of Rome, like as Marius and Sulla, started having an outsized impact on politics. Because of their military victories, they were able to gain enormous authority, which they then exploited to influence politics and threaten the established republican order.

- The Dictatorship of Sulla: Sulla's conquest of Rome in 82 BC and his ensuing dictatorship demonstrated the fragility of the Roman political order.

During the reign of the First Triumvirate,

In order to further their own agendas and consolidate power at the end of the Roman Republic, Julius Caesar, Pompey, and Crassus created a political alliance known as the First Triumvirate. By avoiding the usual routes of government, this secret deal shook up the status quo.

When the First Triumvirate fell apart in 49 B.C. and Caesar crossed the Rubicon, he sparked a civil war that lasted until his dictatorship was overthrown and he was killed in 44 B.C.

II. The Consolidation of Power and the Ascendancy of the Emperors

"The Last Days of the Republic"

Corruption in government, military intervention, and personal ambitions all contributed to the fall of the Roman Republic. The conventional republican structure collapsed after the assassination of Julius Caesar and the subsequent fight for control.

After Caesar's death, Octavian (later Augustus), Mark Antony, and Lepidus formed the Second Triumvirate. The goal of this coalition was to avenge Caesar's death and gain political control.

Principate 2:

After the fall of the Second Triumvirate, a power struggle ensued, and Augustus, the grandnephew of Julius Caesar, eventually came out on top. He instituted the Principate, which gave the appearance of being a Roman Republic government while actually consolidating power in the hands of the emperor.

Maintaining a steady state The Pax Romana, a time of peace and prosperity, began with Augustus and lasted as long as he was in power. His succession planning helped keep the new government in place.

The Third Century of the Julio-Claudian Dynasty: Difficulties and Uncertainty

Problems with Succession 1.

The succession of emperors became a problem for the Julio-Claudian dynasty after the death of Augustus in 14 AD. Uncertainty and bad leadership choices were common results of the convoluted system of adoption and marriage alliances.

Both Emperors Tiberius and Caligula were accused of tyranny and exhibited unstable behaviour during their reigns. Political unrest and widespread dissatisfaction were exacerbated by their leadership.

Second, "The Year of the Four Emperors":

After Nero's death and the subsequent anarchy in the Roman Empire, 69 AD became known as the "Year of the Four Emperors." Civil war and political instability ensued as each of Galba, Otho, Vitellius, and Vespasian claimed the throne in fast succession.

- The Rise of Vespasian: Vespasian prevailed, establishing the Flavian dynasty and restoring some stability to the Roman Empire.

The Third Century Crisis: Internal Strife and Upheaval

1. Anarchy in the Military:

The Third Century Crisis (AD 235-284) was a time of great unrest and anarchy in the Roman Empire. Several Roman emperors came and went, sometimes in rapid succession, as the Roman army and frontier provinces fought for their own autonomy.

A succession of military leaders, often referred to as the "barracks emperors," assumed control during this era. Their lifespans were frequently cut short by barbarian invasions.

2. The Breakup of the Roman Empire:

During the third-century Crisis, the empire broke up into various territories, each of which had its own ruler. During this time, tensions between the Western Roman Empire and the Eastern Roman Empire (also known as the Byzantine Empire) grew.

The decline of the empire's economy brought about by factors such as currency devaluation and widespread inflation.

Legacy and Teachings

Ancient Rome's political upheaval and succession struggles can teach us a lot:

Roman history teaches us that republican governments are fragile and easily toppled by internal power struggles, corruption, or external military intervention. The importance of stable institutions and processes for peaceful changes of government are highlighted. Powerful leaders were essential to Roman stability and crisis management throughout the empire's history. Instability was often a result of poor leadership.

The difficulty of determining who will succeed the current leader is a constant problem, especially in hereditary monarchies and autocracies. Long-term stability requires well-defined and well-executed succession plans.

Fourth, the difficulty of changing governments needs careful management of institutions, symbols, and public views, as Rome discovered when it switched from the Republic to the Principate.

5. The Effects of Political Unrest: Unrest in government can have far-reaching effects on a nation's citizens, economy, and national defence. The lessons that can be learned from Rome's past can help other countries who are going through tough times.

The instability of ancient Roman politics and the succession crises that plagued the empire are examples of the difficulties in leading and being ambitious human beings and the inherent instability of political structures. The Roman Empire was plagued by internal instability and external dangers despite its impressive cultural, legal, and engineering achievements. Lessons and insights about the difficulties of leadership, governance, and the preservation of political stability in a diverse and dynamic community can be gleaned from Rome's history.

3.3. External threats, including barbarian invasions

Rome's Dangerous Frontiers Facing Foreign Threats and Barbarian Invasions

The power, resilience, and ability to defend the empire's enormous frontiers were all put to the test during ancient Rome's history, which is marked not only by its extraordinary achievements but also by the continual external threats and barbarian invasions. Rome's expansionist goals and territorial holdings made it a target for numerous tribes, nations, and confederations who sought to challenge her dominance. We will investigate the causes, effects, and lasting lessons offered by the foreign dangers and barbarian invasions that provided tremendous challenges to the Roman Empire.

I. Rome's porous borders present a geographical challenge.

Large Open Spaces:

The Roman Empire was characterised by its vast territory, which spanned from Britain in the west to Mesopotamia in the east. Defence and administration were made more difficult by the sheer size of this area.

The northern and eastern borders of the empire were particularly exposed to outside attacks due to their proximity to the Rhine and Danube rivers. The absence of natural defences made the imperial territory even more vulnerable.

The Limes, Second Line of Defence

The limes were a series of Roman fortifications built to protect the city's borders. Walls, watchtowers, and fortifications were strategically erected along the borders to protect the territory.

Hadrian's Wall was constructed by the Romans as a protective barrier between Britain and the northern tribes of Picts and Scots.

The Danube Limes were a string of forts and strongholds built along the Danube to keep an eye on the frontier and keep things under control.

Part Two: The Danger from Foreign Barbarians

The First Group, the Savages:

In ancient Rome, "barbarian" was a pejorative word for anyone who wasn't Roman or Greek. There were several independent kingdoms and tribal confederations beyond the borders of the Roman Empire, each with its own language, customs, and history.

North and east of the Roman Empire were lands inhabited by Germanic peoples like the Goths, Vandals, and Suebi.

The Parthians and their successors, the Sassanids, presented problems along the empire's eastern border.

Second, the time of migration:

The Migration Era (or Völkerwanderung) was a time of great upheaval and dislocation for several indigenous peoples in Europe. Mass migrations and invasions were common throughout this time, which spans the late 4th and early 6th centuries A.D.

A major external threat arose in the form of the Huns, a nomadic confederation from the Eurasian steppes. Other tribal tribes, such as the Goths and Vandals, were forced into Roman territory as a result of their invasions in the late 4th and 5th century AD.
In 406 A.D., a group of Germanic tribes made headlines when they invaded Roman Gaul by navigating the icy Rhine River.

Major Invasions and Their Repercussions

During the first Gothic War (376–382):

The Gothic War was a protracted struggle that began when the Visigoths (a subgroup of the Goths) invaded Roman territory. The Romans had a tough time accommodating the Visigoths' complaints and demands for territory and resources.

The Battle of Adrianople, which took place in 378 AD, was a watershed event. The Romans lost horribly, and Emperor Valens was murdered in action.

Conflict was resolved in 382 A.D. when the Visigoths were awarded territory within the empire in exchange for their military service. This was a precursor to the incorporation of savage soldiers into the Roman army.

Attacks by Vandals (439–442 AD)

The Vandals were a Germanic people who invaded North Africa and eventually became the dominant power there. Carthage, a great city and an important supply of grain for Rome, was taken by them in 439 A.D.

The Western Roman Empire's economy suffered greatly as a result of the loss of North Africa. The Vandals' destruction of Rome's grain transport system exacerbated the city's chronic food scarcity.

The Visigoths' 410 A.D. sack of Rome:
Rome fell to the Visigoths in 410 A.D. under King Alaric. It had been nearly 800 years since the city had been sacked by an outside enemy, therefore this occurrence caused a sensation in the ancient world. The sack of Rome was a metaphor for the collapse and centralization of the Western Roman Empire.

IV. Takeaways and Impact Several valuable lessons can be drawn from the Roman Empire's experiences with foreign threats and barbarian invasions:

As an example of the first vulnerability of large empires, Rome's extensive territorial holdings made it difficult to properly protect its boundaries. This weakness highlights the difficulty of administering and protecting expansive empires.

The Limestone Requirements of Border Defence (2): The need of strategic planning and defensive infrastructure in dealing with external threats is demonstrated by Rome's reliance on fortifications like the limes. The Huns and other nomadic peoples showed how powerfully disruptive mobile, cavalry-based armies might be. Nomadic soldiers' ability to cover enormous distances and penetrate deep into Roman territory was a new and dangerous factor.

Significant economic and population declines resulted from external invasions and threats. The disruption of the Roman economy caused by the loss of key provinces like North Africa hastened the decline of the Roman Empire.

5. Lessons in Adaptation: As the political situation shifted, the Romans were compelled to adapt by enlisting barbarian armies. Despite its flaws, this approach was useful in dealing with a lack of personnel. The external dangers and barbarian invasions that ancient Rome endured were, in the end, fundamental to the downfall of the empire. These tests provide a plethora of information about the difficulties of empire management, the precariousness of frontier areas, and the flexibility of response in times of crisis. The history of Rome's struggles against outsiders is instructive because it highlights the dynamic factors that determine the course of nations and civilizations, and it continues to shed light on the ever-present difficulties encountered by empires and states.

Chapter 4:
"Western Roman Empire's Decline"

4.1. Economic decline and overextension

The fall of the Roman Empire can be attributed to economic decline and overextension.

At its height, the Roman Empire encompassed much of the known ancient world over three continents and exerted tremendous influence. But its decline and fall were the product of a complicated interaction of economic causes and overextension, not a single catastrophic event. In this investigation, we will examine the reasons, effects, and lessons to be learned from the economic collapse and overextension that lead to the fall of the Roman Empire.

I. Increasing Wealth and Business Opportunities

1: The Economic Base:

Agriculture, trade, and industry all contributed to the Roman Empire's prosperous economy. The empire's hegemony over the Mediterranean's rich agricultural soil allowed it to produce vast quantities of food.

The surplus food production of the empire provided for its people and also served as a source of revenue thanks to exports.

To promote the free flow of products, ideas, and culture, Rome set up huge trading networks that reached from the Middle East to Europe.

Second, Accumulating Wealth:
   The Roman Empire was immensely wealthy and powerful as a result of its conquest of new regions like Gaul, Britain, and Egypt.

The monetary success of the empire owed much to the conquest of these areas.

The Roman imperial treasury was bolstered by the tribute and taxes paid by the newly conquered provinces.

Rome's resources were bolstered by the tribute given by client states it maintained. These states either paid a tax or offered military support.

Economic Decline Indicators, Part II

1. Depreciation of the currency:

Currency depreciation, especially by debasement of its coins, was a persistent problem for the Roman Empire. Lack of faith in the monetary system was exacerbated by the excessive minting of coins with depleted precious metal content.

Currency devaluation contributed to inflation, which in turn made it harder for the general public to afford basic necessities.

Costly Taxes

High rates of taxation were required to fund the massive territorial holdings and military campaigns of the Roman Empire. Farmers were already struggling to make ends meet before taxes were collected in the form of their goods.

Provinces, especially those that were exploited extensively, paid a disproportionate share of federal taxes. Costly tribute demands have the potential to destroy local economies.

Thirdly, Economic Disparity:

The Roman Empire had severe economic inequality. The affluent elite, known as patricians, controlled the majority of the country's wealth and resources, while the plebeians and slaves made up the rest of the population and had few economic options.

The redistribution of land and the availability of farmland were perennial issues. The elite resisted reforms to land ownership, such as the Gracchi brothers' planned Lex Agraria.

Thirdly, Excessive Expansion: The Weight of Huge Territories

First, Military Overextension:

The Roman military was tasked with enforcing order throughout a massive territory spanning many continents. The military was stretched extremely thin by the necessity to protect the borders and keep the peace in outlying regions.

Long military campaigns, especially those conducted in areas outside the empire's heart, necessitated a great deal of supplies and troops.

Challenges of loyalty and discipline arose when the Roman Empire became increasingly reliant on mercenaries and auxiliary troops recruited from non-Roman people.

Limits That Cannot Be Crossed

The Roman Empire faced difficulties in defending and securing its vast frontiers, especially along the Rhine and Danube rivers. It was difficult to strengthen and guard every weak spot along the borders because of their sheer size.

Rome's enemies came from all directions: the Parthians in the east, the Germanic tribes in the north, and others besides. Constant awareness and resources were necessary for managing these dangers.

Consequences of Economic Decline and Overextension

Economic Weakness (1):

Currency devaluation, excessive taxes, and widespread economic inequality all contributed to the empire's economic decline. Financial instability made it difficult to meet the fundamental requirements of the populace and maintain a strong defence.

Second, social unrest:

Unrest and discontent among the Roman citizens was fueled by economic inequality and high taxes. As the economy deteriorated, demonstrations, riots, and uprisings multiplied.

Dangers from Without:

Invasions and attacks from outsiders like the Visigoths, Vandals, and Huns took advantage of the empire's fragility. Rome's defences were ineffective, leading to territory losses.

Disintegration (4th):

The collapse in the Roman Empire's economy and its overextension both had a role in its eventual disintegration. Multiple provinces of the empire, each controlled by a different emperor, emerged from the Crisis of the Third Century.

Legacy and Teachings

Lessons can be learned from the Roman Empire's economic collapse and overextension:

The Roman Empire's expansion into vast new regions was successful, but it also contained the germs of its own destruction. The difficulty comes from trying to sustainably expand without draining resources.

Second, a stable economy is essential to an empire's continued existence. Controlling inflation, tax rates, and economic disparity are all crucial elements of any functioning economy.

economic security.

Thirdly, military strategy, which includes the distribution of resources and the defence of sensitive frontiers, is essential for the management of a huge empire.

4. Social Cohesion: Maintaining order and preventing social unrest depend on social cohesion and resolving the problems of the public.

The longevity of every empire depends on leadership that can adjust to new conditions as they arise. When a society fails to adjust to new economic conditions or external threats, it can stagnate and even break apart.

Last but not least, the Roman Empire's economic collapse and overextension demonstrate the dangers that can afflict even the most advanced societies. The decline of Rome was due to a number of factors working together, including economic instability, overexpansion, and external threats. The lessons that can be drawn from Rome's demise remain instructive for current states and empires as they attempt to deal with the intricacies of politics, economy, and defence in today's interconnected world.

4.2. Military challenges and internal strife

The Roman Empire fell apart due to military threats and civil strife.

History tells us that the once-mighty Roman Empire was weakened throughout time by a variety of military threats and internal unrest. For centuries, the Roman legions were the backbone of Roman authority. However, the empire's resources, leadership, and cohesion were all taxed by a variety of external threats and internal strife. This inquiry sheds insight on the origins, outcomes, and lasting lessons of the military problems and internal unrest that significantly contributed to the fall of the Roman Empire.

Roman Military Technology, Part I

"The Legions"

It was well-known that the Roman legions were exceptionally well-trained and organised. To conquer and keep control of such enormous territory, the Roman military relied on these professional troops.

Training was rigorous, emphasising discipline and loyalty, and Roman citizens were expected to serve in the legions.

- Standardised weapons and armour were just the beginning; the Romans also used cutting-edge tactics and engineering in their wars.

Dangers from Without:

Rome's expansion into new territories made it vulnerable to attacks from many other countries and people groups.
Rome's rival in the east was the Parthian Empire (later the Sassanid Empire), with whom it fought on and off for years to determine who would rule over Mesopotamia.

The northern frontiers of the Roman Empire along the Rhine and Danube rivers were constantly threatened by invading Germanic tribes such as the Goths and Vandals.

The Visigothic sack of Rome in 410 AD was just one example of a barbarian invasion that demonstrated how vulnerable Rome's boundaries were.

II. Civil War and Political Uncertainty

Crisis of Succession 1.

Succession problems plagued the Roman Empire, especially in its twilight years. Conflict and intrigue frequently hampered the handoff of power from one emperor to the next.

The struggle for the imperial crown was marked by assassinations, usurpations, and military coups.

- Competing Emperors: Disputes and conflicts broke out within the empire when there were rivals for the throne.

The Third Century Crisis

During the third century AD, known as the Crisis of the Third Century, the Roman Empire was shaken to its foundations by a series of emperor changes, imperial disintegration, and foreign invasions.

It was a time of relative chaos in the armed forces, with "barracks emperors" rising to power and then falling quickly.

The empire suffered territory losses at this time, with the Gallic and Palmyrene kingdoms emerging as independent states.

The Third Recession:

Currency depreciation, high taxes, and economic inequality all contributed to the country's internal struggle and social discontent.

Protests, riots, and revolts arose out of the Roman populace's anger with economic disparity and high taxation.

Rome's reliance on mercenaries and other non-Roman auxiliary troops exacerbated loyalty and discipline problems within the army.

The Most Important Military Challenges and Their Repercussions

One, during the Gothic Wars (376–382 AD):

A series of wars known as the Gothic Wars broke out when the Visigoths moved into Eastern Roman territory.

The Battle of Adrianople, which took place in 378 AD, was a watershed moment in history. The Romans lost horribly, and Emperor Valens was murdered in action.

A change in the distribution of power occurred with the Treaty of 382, which gave the Visigoths territories within the empire.

Sassanid Conflicts, 224–363 A.D.

In the east, the Sassanid Empire (the successor to the Parthian Empire) and the Roman Empire fought multiple wars over Mesopotamia and Armenia.

As a result of the Sassanian Wars, the Roman Empire had less money and fewer troops to defend its other borders.

The Third Century Crisis (AD 234–284):
External invasions, civil wars, and internal struggle all contributed to the empire's weakening during the Crisis of the Third Century.

Internal instability was compounded by the empire's fragmentation into smaller territories ruled by rival emperors. Tribal tribes such as the Goths, Vandals, and Huns launched barbarian invasions against the empire, taking advantage of its depleted strength.

IV. Takeaways and Impact Several valuable lessons can be drawn from the military difficulties and internal unrest that plagued the Roman Empire:

Leadership and Succession 1: The stability of any government or empire depends on the ability to secure a seamless and legitimate succession of power.

Second, a state needs economic stability to thrive in the long run. Social unrest and a country's ability to defend itself are possible outcomes of high taxes, currency devaluation, and economic disparity.

protect itself. Military planning, resource management, and flexibility are essential components of border defence since they allow for the administration of large boundaries and the protection of frontiers. The vastness and complexity of the Roman Empire left it vulnerable to both internal unrest and external assaults, illustrating the fragility of large systems. For complex systems to be resilient, strong mechanisms are required.

5. The Importance of Leadership Strong leadership is crucial in trying times. Ineffective or corrupt leadership contributed to Rome's military difficulties and internal unrest.

As a result of military threats and internal unrest, the Roman Empire gradually declined and eventually collapsed. Understanding the difficulties of leadership, defence, and administration in a world where nations and empires are constantly tested by external and internal challenges is made possible by the lessons learnt from this historical experience, which remain applicable to this day. The lasting challenges and the repercussions of civilizations' responses are illustrated by Rome's legacy.

4.3. The fall of the Western Roman Empire

The Decline and Fall of the Western Roman Empire and the Origins of the Modern World.

The decline of the Western Roman Empire and the beginning of the Middle Ages in Europe are two of the most consequential events in human history. Multiple internal and external reasons contributed to the severe fall and final demise of the Western Roman Empire in the late 5th century AD. In this investigation, we will delve into the complex history of the decline of the Western Roman Empire, analysing its origins, major events, and lasting impact.

I. The Perilous Late Roman Empire

The Breakup of the Political System

Multiple emperors were competing for control of the Roman Empire by the fourth century AD. As time went on, the chasm that separated the Eastern and Western Roman Empires widened.

By moving the capital from Rome to Byzantium (Constantinople) in the early 4th century, Emperor Constantine signalled the eastward shift in the dominance of the empire by instituting substantial reforms.

During the Crisis of the Third Century, the empire was ruled by a series of short-lived emperors, many of whom were military commanders.

Economic Pressure 2:

Currency devaluation, inflation, and an over-reliance on slave labour were just a few of the problems that plagued the Roman economy. The economic strain was exacerbated by excessive taxation and widespread corruption.

Due to soil degradation and excessive use of slave labour, agricultural productivity fell, which negatively impacted food production.

The constant incursions of hostile tribes into the empire's territory exacerbated the economic situation.

II. The External Threat and the Role of the Barbarians

1. Invasion by Savages:

The Visigoths, Vandals, Huns, and Ostrogoths were just some of the tribes that repeatedly attacked the Western Roman Empire.

The Visigoths, under Alaric's leadership, seized and plundered Rome in 410 AD, dealing a severe blow to Roman dignity.

Food shortages at Rome were caused by the Vandals, who founded a kingdom in North Africa and hampered the empire's grain supply.

The Huns under Attila:

Under Attila's leadership, the Huns, a nomadic confederation from the Eurasian steppes, posed a significant danger to the Western Roman Empire.

Attila's invasions in the middle of the fifth century damaged the empire's defences and led to its instability.
Attila's advance was stopped at the decisive Battle of the Catalaunian Plains (451 AD) by the Roman general Aetius and the Visigothic king Theodoric I.

Internal Conflict and Political Uncertainty

Crisis of Succession 1.

It wasn't uncommon for the handover of power from one emperor to the next to be fraught with intrigue and violence. Throughout the late Roman Empire, assassinations, usurpations, and military coups were typical occurrences.

- Competing Emperors: Civil wars and internal struggle resulted from times when there were competing claimants to the imperial throne.

A number of usurpers, like Magnus Maximus and Eugenius, rose to power and attempted to steal control of the Roman Empire.

Second, social unrest:

Discontent and social unrest among the Roman citizens stemmed from economic inequality and high taxes. Protests, riots, and uprisings happened more frequently.

The Bagaudae Uprisings were started by bands of farmers who were fed up with high taxes and exploitation.

Factors that Contributed to the Downfall (IV)

One, the last emperor of Rome (476 A.D.)

In 476 AD, a Germanic leader named Odoacer toppled the last Roman emperor, Romulus Augustulus, marking a watershed moment for the Western Roman Empire.
As a result of Odoacer's actions, the Western Roman Empire no longer had a native Roman emperor, marking the symbolic end of the empire.

After the fall of the Roman Empire, Germanic Kingdoms arose.

After Romulus Augustulus was deposed, the Western Roman Empire disintegrated into a loose confederation of Germanic states.

The Western Roman Empire collapsed, while Odoacer's client kingship over Italy continued under the Eastern Roman Empire.

The Byzantine Empire, which had its capital in Constantinople, carried on as the Eastern Roman Empire and kept its grip over the Eastern Mediterranean.

Theodoric and the Kingdom of the Ostrogoths:

Despite being an Ostrogoth, Theodoric the Great became king of an Italian state that was subject to the Eastern Roman Empire.

Under Theodoric's leadership, relations between the Romans and the Goths stabilised and even improved.

The Decline and Fall of the Vandal Kingdom and Carthage

The Vandals conquered Carthage in 439 A.D., cutting off the Western Roman Empire from its main source of grain.

The Roman economy was thrown into disarray and food shortages exacerbated by the loss of North Africa.

Legacy and Teachings

The collapse of
Several valuable lessons can be learned from the Western Roman Empire:

1. Political Fragmentation: The empire's ability to respond to external threats and internal difficulties was hindered due to the empire's division and fragmentation.

The longevity of an empire depends on its economy remaining stable. Economic disparity, currency depreciation, and excessive taxes all contribute to societal discontent.

Third, military preparedness is essential, as the persistent pressure from outside threats has shown.

Fourth, good leadership and administration are indispensable in emergency situations. A state's downfall can be hastened by weak or corrupt leadership, which can in turn aggravate internal unrest.

The Eastern Roman Empire, or Byzantine Empire, endured for centuries and preserved many features of Roman society, including its legal and administrative systems.

In conclusion, a new period had begun in European history with the fall of the Western Roman Empire. The Roman world was transformed as a result of centuries of struggle against both internal and external threats. Rome's decline is a cautionary story of the intricate interplay of forces that can lead to the unravelling of even the mightiest of empires, and its legacy lives on via its contributions to art, culture, governance, and law.

Chapter 5:
"The Continuation of the Roman Empire in the East"

5.1. The Byzantine Empire and its capital, Constantinople

A Story of Persistence and Progress: Constantinople and the Byzantine Empire

The Byzantine Empire, often known as the Eastern Roman Empire, lasted for more than a thousand years after the decline of the Western Roman Empire. Constantinople was the beating heart of this enduring empire, and it was an extremely important city for both ancient and modern reasons. As we dig into the history of the Byzantine Empire and its capital, Constantinople, we will learn about their fascinating beginnings, evolution, cultural contributions, and enduring legacies.

I. Constantinople's Beginnings

A. The Breakup of the Roman Empire B.

A major turning point in Roman history occurred when Emperor Diocletian split the empire in two, creating the Eastern and Western portions, in the late 3rd century AD. Byzantium, capital of the Eastern Roman Empire, became the foundation of what would become known as the Byzantine Empire.

Second, Constantine's Prophecy:

The city of Constantinople owes much to the efforts of Emperor Constantine the Great, who ruled from 306 to 337 AD. On the ruins of Byzantium, he established Constantinople as the new imperial capital in 324 AD.

The strategic location of Constantinople, straddling the Bosporus Strait between Europe and Asia, gave it an inherent advantage in defence and made international trade much simpler.

Greek influence: Constantine's decision to move the capital eastward reflected the empire's growing importance of the Greek-speaking provinces.

The Byzantine Empire Part II: Stability and Change

Keeping the Same Management Team:

Much of the Roman Empire's administrative organisation and judicial traditions were adopted by the Byzantine Empire. This consistency allowed for the effective administration of large areas.

Byzantine legal systems such as the Justinian Code were preserved because of the Byzantines' adherence to Roman legal ideas.

The Byzantine bureaucracy was efficient because it was structured on the idea of "themes," which also aided in taxation and government.

Second, the Empire's Christianization:

The Byzantine Empire was crucial to the growth and dissemination of Christianity. Christianity was officially recognised by the Roman Empire after being declared legal by Emperor Constantine.

Christian doctrine was shaped by ecumenical councils held in the Byzantine Empire, including the First Council of Nicaea in 325 and the Council of Chalcedon in 451.

The Hagia Sophia, one of the world's most recognisable churches, was built using cutting-edge techniques that attested to the faith and engineering of the Byzantine Empire.

3. Accomplishments in the Arts:

The Byzantine Empire contributed important contributions to Western culture, especially in the visual arts, literature, and philosophy.

Intricate mosaics, frescoes, and holy icons are typical of Byzantine art, which is typically displayed in places of worship.

Byzantine scholars worked to preserve and copy ancient Greek and Roman manuscripts, protecting a treasure trove of information.

Reconquests under Justinian, Part 4:

Byzantine Emperor Justinian I (527–565) led a series of military battles to retake areas that had fallen to invaders.

Successfully retaking North Africa and parts of Italy, Justinian's soldiers briefly reunified a large chunk of the Western Roman Empire.

Third, the Iconoclast Debate

Iconoclasm, No. 1:

about the course of several centuries, a heated debate raged about the appropriateness of using religious icons, especially in Christian liturgy.

Some Byzantine emperors, known as iconoclasts, encouraged the destruction of religious images because they believed that worshipping them amounted to idolatry.

However, Iconophiles opposed these ideas, arguing that icons play an important role in bringing believers closer to God.
Second, "The Orthodox Conquest":

Byzantine icons were officially reinstated when the "Triumph of Orthodoxy" in 843 AD ended the Iconoclast Controversy.

Iconoclasm and the veneration of icons were both upheld and condemned by the Seventh Ecumenical Council (the Second Council of Nicaea).

Part Four: Adjacent States to the Byzantine Empire

First, the State of U.S.-Iran Ties

Both war and diplomacy were part of the ongoing connection between the Sassanian (later Persian) Empire and the Byzantine Empire.

Wars waged between the Byzantine Empire and the Persian Empire over the territories of Mesopotamia and Armenia depleted resources and led to changes in territorial boundaries.

- The "Eternal Peace": The Treaty of Eternal Peace in 532 AD temporarily ended hostilities and established the Euphrates River as the border between the two empires.

Second, the Muslim-Christian War

The advent of Islam in the seventh century AD presented the Byzantine Empire with a serious threat. Land in the Levant and North Africa was lost to the Byzantine Empire after the Arab-Byzantine Wars broke out in the seventh century.

One of the greatest defensive successes of the Roman Empire was achieved during the Arab siege of Constantinople (717–718).

The Demise of Byzantium and the Legacy of Constantinople
One, the Conquest of the Ottomans:

The fall of Constantinople to the Ottomans in 1453 marked the end of the Byzantine Empire. The successful siege led by Mehmed the Conqueror was the beginning of Ottoman domination and the end of Byzantine sovereignty.

The fall of Constantinople left a significant imprint on European and Middle Eastern history as a whole, notably the spread of Byzantine knowledge to the West.
What the Byzantines Gave to the Renaissance

Beyond its borders, the Byzantine Empire left an enduring legacy. After the fall of Constantinople, many Byzantine scholars and texts made their way to the West, where they were instrumental in fostering the intellectual growth that led to the Renaissance.

Knowledge Transmission: Classical Greek and Roman writings were preserved and transmitted by Byzantine scholars, who played a crucial role in the Renaissance of learning in Europe.

3. Inheritance in Art and Architecture: The Byzantine Empire's influence on Eastern Orthodox Christian art and architecture was profound. For instance, the Hagia Sophia is still standing as an example of Byzantine architectural advancements.

Eastern Orthodox Christianity is profoundly influenced by Byzantine religious practises and traditions.
Overall, the Byzantine Empire and its seat of power, Constantinople, hold a singular position in the annals of humankind. Their history includes developments in government, culture, and religion, but also shows continuity with the ancient world. The decline of the empire in 1453 signalled the end of an age, but its legacy lived on in the form of knowledge that was preserved and passed on, as well as in the form of the Renaissance and the Eastern Orthodox Christian tradition. The capital city of this once-great empire, Constantinople, has become a universal icon of the Byzantine legacy.

5.2. Justinian and the reconquest of the Western Empire

The Complex Legacy of Justinian's Victorious Reconquest of the Western Empire

Many historians consider Emperor Justinian I (527–565) to be among the most powerful and ambitious Byzantine emperors. During his rule, key provinces of the Western Roman Empire, such as Italy and North Africa, were reclaimed. The military wars, legislative reforms, and cultural triumphs of the Byzantine Empire's growth during this time period are what give it its name, the Justinianic Reconquest. This investigation will dive into the life and reign of Emperor Justinian I, the causes of the reconquest, and the lasting effects of that time.

I. Justinian's Childhood and Early Career

The Beginning:

In 482, in the town of Tauresium in Illyria (present-day North Macedonia), Justinian entered the world. He was born into a poor family yet managed to get a good education.

His uncle Justin I, who had worked as a palace guard before becoming Emperor Justin I in 518 AD, was a major influence on Justinian. The importance of this family tie to Justinian's ascent to power cannot be overstated.

Succession and Co-Emperorship:

In 527 AD, Justinian's uncle Justin I appointed him co-emperor, making him the de facto ruler of the empire.

After Justin I's untimely demise in 527 A.D., Justinian ascended to the throne and began a long and fruitful reign that was characterised by greatness and invention.

Justinian's Legal Reforms, Part 2

One, the Roman codification of law:

Codifying Roman law was one of Justinian's most significant contributions to history. He hired a group of lawyers, headed by the jurist Tribonian, to collect and codify the preexisting legal codes into a single document.

- Justinian's Code: The resultant corpus of law, the Corpus Juris Civilis (Body of Civil Law), comprised the Digest, the Institutes, and the Code, all of which became seminal works in the evolution of Western legal systems.

By codifying and clarifying Roman law, Justinian laid the groundwork for the development of contemporary legal systems across Europe.

Restructuring the Bureaucracy

Many administrative changes were made during Justinian's reign in an effort to make government more open and efficient.

- Bureaucratic Restructuring: To improve governance, Justinian reorganised the Byzantine bureaucracy and instituted novel administrative procedures.

He aimed to bring back and keep alive historic Roman institutions, stressing the need of being true to the past.

Third, Justinian's Military Efforts
The First War with the Vandals (532–534):
The Vandalic War, fought against a Germanic tribe that had established a kingdom in North Africa, was one of Justinian's earliest significant military battles.

In order to restore Roman power in North Africa, Justinian entrusted the skilled general Belisarius with the war that resulted in the capture of Carthage.

Importance: The victory over the Vandals was a major step towards fulfilling Justinian's territorial goals.

Second, during the Gothic War (535–554 AD):

The Gothic War against the Ostrogoths, who ruled Italy and had a fragile grip on Rome, was Justinian's most significant military operation.

Belisarius and Narses: Belisarius played a critical role once more, leading Byzantine armies to victory and the conquest of strategic cities like Rome. Even after Belisarius had left, the campaign lasted until it was finally won by the eunuch general Narses.

Italy was reunified under Byzantine power after the Gothic War, however the Byzantine Empire only held sway over Italian territory for a brief period of time.

Third, Rome Is Retaken

The retaking of Rome by Belisarius in 536 A.D. was a watershed moment in the Gothic War. But the city's population and clout had declined since the glory days of the Roman Empire.

War, plague, and population loss over many years had taken a toll on the once-proud metropolis, and its lustre had faded.

Reconquest Obstacles and Expenses
Stress from Money Matters

Although sometimes fruitful, military battles often came at a high cost. Justinian's objectives required him to impose enormous taxes on his subjects, which often resulted in economic misery for them.

Outbreaks of bubonic plague and bouts of famine also put a strain on the empire's resources.

2. Geographical Restriction:

Parts of the Western Roman Empire, including North Africa and Italy, were retaken by Justinian, but he was unable to maintain his control over these regions for very long.

- Uncertainty and Reversals: Both North Africa and Italy experienced times of unrest before falling to the Visigoths and the Lombards, respectively.

Justinian's Legacy and the Reconquest

1. Inheritance in Law and Culture:

By codifying his legal changes in what is now known as the Justinian Code, Justinian left an imprint on the legal systems of Europe and beyond.

Significant advancements in Byzantine art and architecture, such as the building of the Hagia Sophia, were also made during Justinian's reign.

In-Depth Analysis of Past Events:

The historical significance of Justinian's reign is debatable. His bold reconquests were impressive, but they were expensive and frequently failed.

While some historians praise Justinian as a visionary who worked to restore Rome to its former splendour, others point out the negative effects of his policies on the economy and political stability.

Justinian's legacy lives on through the legal reforms he instituted and the contributions he made to Byzantine culture, notwithstanding the controversy surrounding his reign.

In sum, the reign of Justinian and the Justinianic Reconquest were a watershed moment in the development of the Byzantine Empire, full of unprecedented complexity and ambitious accomplishment. His influence on Byzantine law and culture, and on Western civilisation more generally, was profound. The military campaigns were effective, but they were costly and sensitive to historical tides. The reign of Justinian is an example of how one person may have a profound effect on the development of an entire empire and beyond.

5.3. Byzantine contributions to art, culture, and law

Legacy of Byzantine Innovation and Preservation in the Arts, Sciences, and Law

Despite being eclipsed by the Roman Empire in the West, the Byzantine Empire left a lasting cultural and legal legacy. Byzantium, a fusion of Greco-Roman culture with Eastern influences and Christian piety, was a beacon of civilization in the Eastern Mediterranean for more than a thousand years. This study dives into the diverse fabric of Byzantine contributions, analysing seminal works, formative influences, and the amazing civilization's ongoing legacy.

Byzantine Art I. Blending of Old and New

First, the use of icons:

Religious icons, in particular, are among the most well-known examples of Byzantine art. Byzantine religious life revolved around these elaborate and spiritually charged paintings on wood or other materials.

- Religious Importance: Icons were seen as portals to the sacred and the sublime, affording a glimpse of the divine.

The Iconoclastic Controversy was sparked by the widespread use of iconography and lasted for centuries before being settled in favour of iconophiles.

Tile mosaics:

Beautiful mosaics were frequently used to decorate Byzantine basilicas and churches. Mosaics often depicted scenes from the Bible or the lives of the saints, and they were elaborate in design and brimming with colour.

The Hagia Sophia in Constantinople (now Istanbul) is home to some of the most well-known Byzantine mosaics, notably the Christ Pantocrator and Virgin Mary-decorated heavenly dome.

Symbolism of the Christian faith and theology was often depicted in mosaics alongside its creative manifestation.

The Third: Buildings

Byzantine design fused aspects of Western and Eastern styles. The splendour of the empire was on display in the form of basilicas, cathedral domes, and other massive buildings.

Byzantine architects were masters at constructing domes, and these structures became an iconic feature of ancient cityscapes.

The Italian city of Ravenna, which was ruled by the Byzantines for a short time, is famous for its many surviving examples of Byzantine mosaics and architecture.

The Byzantines as Keepers of Language and History

1. The Safekeeping of Ancient Texts

The literary and philosophical works of the ancient world were preserved in large part because to the efforts of Byzantine intellectuals. Classical literature were stored in monasteries and libraries to protect them from being lost or destroyed.

Many ancient books were translated into Greek, and commentary and analyses by Byzantine scholars aided in our comprehension of those translations.

The works of ancient intellectuals like Ptolemy, Euclid, and Aristotle were saved and studied, influencing subsequent Western thought during the Renaissance. - Ptolemaic Knowledge.

Second, Greek literature and language:

Greek became the dominant language of the Byzantine Empire, while Latin remained the official language of the Western Roman Empire.

Byzantine philosophers like John Damascene and Michael Psellos had a role in carrying on the work of ancient Greek thinkers.

Some of the most influential historical accounts of Byzantine life and politics were written by Byzantine historians like Procopius and Anna Comnena.

The Justinian Code (of Byzantine Law)

One, the Roman codification of law:

Under Emperor Justinian I, Roman law was formally codified for the first time in history. One of the most enduring contributions of Byzantine law is the Justinian Code, often known as the Corpus Juris Civilis.

- Codification of Laws: Under Tribonian's direction, a group of legal experts collected and codified all of the preexisting Roman laws into a single document.

The Justinian Code was instrumental in shaping European law and is considered by many to be the cornerstone of contemporary civil law.

Restructuring the Bureaucracy

During his reign, Justinian also instituted changes to the bureaucracy that would improve government efficiency.

The Byzantine bureaucracy was reorganised to boost administrative effectiveness, tax collection, and provincial administration.

The idea of Byzantine continuity with the ancient world was bolstered by Justinian's efforts to uphold the institutions of Roman rule.

Orthodoxy and Religious Influence

First, Christian Doctrine:

By convening multiple ecumenical councils that dealt with theological disagreements and established essential doctrinal concepts, the Byzantine Empire played a pivotal role in the evolution of Christian theology.

The Nicene Creed and other Christological issues were discussed at the Councils of Nicaea (325 AD) and Chalcedon (451 AD).

When it comes to the growth and consolidation of Orthodox Christianity, the Byzantine Empire was instrumental.

Second, Church Buildings:

Churches and basilicas built during the Byzantine era were especially rich in religious symbolism and meaning.

- Hagia Sophia: The Hagia Sophia, a symbol of Byzantine spirituality and an architectural masterpiece, was constructed in the fourth century under the reign of Emperor Justinian I.

Mosaics and frescoes depicting biblical stories and theological ideas were commonly used to decorate churches and other religious buildings.

V. Lasting Impact and Heritage

Eastern Orthodox Churches and the Byzantine Tradition

Eastern Orthodoxy is influenced by the theological and cultural traditions of the Byzantine Empire. Eastern Orthodox worship relies heavily on its liturgical traditions, theological formulations, and holy art.

What the Byzantines Gave to the Renaissance

To a large extent, Western Europe owes its intellectual development to the Byzantine Empire, which preserved and transmitted ancient knowledge.

Byzantine scholars and their surviving manuscripts connected the ancient world and the Renaissance era through the rediscovery of classical texts.

Third, Repercussions on Today's Legal Systems

The Justinian Code continues to have an impact on contemporary civil law systems, especially in continental Europe.

Many European countries' legal systems can be traced back to the Roman and Byzantine legal traditions, which are known as civil law.

Finally, the lasting influence of the Byzantine Empire may be seen in the arts, the sciences, and the law. Byzantium produced a significant and lasting legacy that continues to affect the modern world, from the preservation of classical knowledge to the formulation of Roman law and the creation of renowned religious art. Byzantine culture and law continue to be admired for their innovative blending of different traditions, their thirst for knowledge, and their profound spiritual and intellectual depth.

Chapter 6:
"Influence and lasting impact"

6.1. The enduring legacy of Roman law and governance

Roman Law and Government: The Bedrock of Western Civilization

The influence of the Roman Republic and Empire, which together lasted for more than a thousand years, is still being felt today. Their contributions to the fields of law and government have had far-reaching effects on contemporary civilizations. This investigation digs into Roman law and governance's legacy, illuminating its foundational components, their historical development, and their far-reaching and enduring impact on modern legal and political structures.

I. The Constitutional Structure of the Roman Republic

There are twelve tables:

The Twelve Tables, a body of legislation enacted in 450 BC during the early Roman Republic, is widely regarded as the cornerstone of Roman law. These tables covered numerous topics associated with civil law, including property rights and judicial procedures.

All citizens were guaranteed the same legal rights and protections by the Twelve Tables, establishing the notion of legal equality.

Protection of property rights, contracts, and civil procedure are among modern legal concepts that owe a debt to the common law.

Institutions of the Republican Party

Combining features of monarchy, aristocracy, and democracy, the Roman Republic pioneered the concept of a hybrid constitution. A few of the most important ones were the Senate, the popular assemblies, and the judiciary.

The Roman Republic followed a system of separation of powers in which the legislative, executive, and judicial departments each had their own specialised functions.

The concept of checks and balances, fundamental to contemporary democratic regimes, has its origins in Roman administration.

Part Two: The Roman Empire's Political Structure

The First Principate:

The Principate was the imperial-led form of Roman government that emerged as the Republic gave way to the Empire. The first emperor, Augustus, set the standard for imperial rule.

It was a mix of Roman military might, diplomatic skill, and good administration that ensured the long period of peace and stability known as the Pax Romana.

Effective Government and Tax Collection: The Roman Empire established a system of administrative provinces and governors.

2. the Roman Code:

During the Roman Empire, prominent jurists such as Gaius, Ulpian, and Papinian made significant contributions to the evolution of Roman law. The Justinian Code is a comprehensive body of law based on the foundations of Roman law.

- The Justinian Code: The "Corpus Juris Civilis," a compilation of Roman law commissioned by Emperor Justinian I, is a seminal legal treatise that had an impact on legal systems throughout Europe.

The Justinian Code laid the foundation for contemporary civil law systems, which are prevalent throughout continental Europe.

The Roman Legal System and Its Lasting Influence

1. Guiding Laws:

The foundational legal ideas established by Roman law remain the backbone upon which contemporary legal systems are built. Among these are:

The Rule of Law is the principle that laws should be unambiguous, consistent, and uniformly enforced.

Individuals' rights and duties under the law are called "legal personhood," or "personhood."

The evolution of contract law, crucial to the functioning of contemporary economies.

The Roman Legal System, Part 2:

Courts, judges, and lawyers all had their origins in the Roman legal system, which paved the way for the present legal system.

Roman legal education, which frequently included apprenticeship with seasoned jurists, contributed to the growth of the field.

When it comes to the study and application of the law, the writings and interpretations of Roman jurists remain essential resources.

Impact on Today's Legal Structures:

The influence of Roman law, especially in civil law countries, has been extensive and far-reaching. Roman legal concepts have been widely adopted by countries in continental Europe, Latin America, and some portions of Asia.

- Roman-Dutch Law: Roman legal concepts have been influential in shaping South Africa's legal system, which is founded on Roman law.

Canon law, the legal code of the Roman Catholic Church, is based on Roman law and is an essential part of church administration to this day.

The Roman Government's Lasting Impact

First, Organisational Hierarchies:

Provincial administration and the civil service are just two examples of how Roman administrative practises have left an indelible mark on contemporary government structure.

Many contemporary nations still use the system of splitting their territories into administrative regions headed by governors appointed from among the population.

Modern administrative institutions can trace their roots back to the Roman system of bureaucracy and civil service.

2.Representative democracy and the rule of law:

The foundations of representative government, a Roman concept, have affected modern democracies.

Representative democracy, in which citizens vote for representatives who will advocate for their interests, has its origins in ancient Roman republics.
Many contemporary democracies, including the United States, take cues from ancient Roman political ideas and institutions.

Participation in Civic Life

The concept of citizenship in contemporary democracies can be traced back to ancient Roman ideals of civic duty and involvement in public affairs.

The Roman concept of active citizenship, in which every member of the society is endowed with both rights and duties, is still foundational to modern democracies.

Civic education and the development of responsible citizens are cornerstones of contemporary democracies.

In the end, the lasting legacy

The influence of an ancient civilization can be seen in the way Roman law and government continue to shape the present world. Modern cultures and institutions are nevertheless shaped by the ideals of legal equality, the rule of law, and representative government. Justice, good government, and citizen engagement were all highly valued during Roman rule, and these ideas have since influenced the evolution of modern political and judicial systems. As such, Rome's contributions to the building blocks of modern civilisation are evidence of the timeless nature of good ideas.

6.2. Roman architecture and engineering

The Roman Empire's Engineering and Architecture: A Golden Age of Innovation and Magnificence

The Romans left behind some of the most remarkable and long-lasting works of architecture and engineering in the ancient world. Roman engineering and architecture has influenced the look of innumerable buildings around the world and continues to impress modern audiences. In this investigation, we delve into the wonders of Roman architecture and engineering, looking closely at their fundamental components, inventions, and far-reaching effects on the history of architecture and engineering.

I. Roman Architecture's Roots

The Impact of the Etruscans:

The Etruscan culture, which flourished in central Italy before Rome, served as an early source of influence for Roman architecture. Roman architecture took cues from Etruscan vaults, arches, and building practises.

The Arch: The arch, a signature of Roman architecture, has its origins in Etruscan structures.

- The Vault: The Romans perfected the barrel vault and the groyne vault, two types of vaulted constructions, after being inspired by Etruscan architecture and engineering.

Construction Supplies:

The Romans were experts at utilising many different types of construction materials, each with its own set of advantages and disadvantages.

Roman concrete was an adaptable and long-lasting building material comprised of volcanic ash, lime and particles.

Stone: The Romans mined and shaped a variety of stones, including marble and limestone, for use in their buildings, temples, and artwork.

Essential Components of Building Design

Archetype 1:

The arch was a key component in the development of monumental entrances, aqueducts, and bridges in Roman architecture.

The Arch of Titus and the Arch of Constantine in Rome are examples of triumphal arches built to celebrate significant military victories.

Arches were crucial in the building of aqueducts, which carried water from far away and distributed it to cities.

Vault Number Two:

The Romans perfected several different kinds of vaults, such as the semicircular barrel vault and the cross-shaped groyne vault.

The Basilica of Maxentius and Constantine is a good example of a basilica with a vaulted ceiling that creates a sense of spaciousness inside.

The Colosseum in Rome, for example, had a maze of tunnels and rooms under its arena, a type of amphitheatre.

The Third Man: By constructing enormous domes, Roman architects pushed the limits of engineering.

The Pantheon's dome is the biggest unreinforced concrete dome in the world, and its central oculus is an engineering wonder.

The Roman dome served as inspiration for following architectural wonders, including Renaissance and modern domes, due to its innovative design and construction techniques.

Ingenious Constructions, Part III

Aqueducts, No. 1:

Roman aqueducts were a feat of engineering that supplied communities with clean water for uses like bathing, drinking, and cooking.

The Segovia Aqueduct in Segovia, Spain, is an excellent example of Roman engineering.

The French aqueduct Pont du Gard is a prime example of the Romans' capacity to construct mega-bridges.

Bridges and roads:

The Romans constructed a massive system of roads and bridges, known as the Roman road system, to improve transportation and commerce throughout their enormous territory.

One of the first and most well-known Roman highways, the Appian Way linked Rome to the Italian peninsula's southern provinces.

The Ponte Fabricio in Rome is just one example of a Roman bridge that demonstrates sophisticated engineering and sturdy construction.

New Developments in Construction and Technology

Concrete Construction: Opus caementicium, the Roman concrete, was an innovative material that allowed for the construction of massive, long-lasting buildings.

Concrete's natural strength and malleability made it an excellent material for building arches and vaults.

Construction Below the Surface: The Romans utilised concrete to build underwater constructions like bridges and harbours.

Second, The Cornerstone and Voussoir:

The keystone was used to secure the other stones (voussoirs) in position when building Roman arches and vaults.

The keystone helped keep the arch stable by distributing the structure's weight uniformly.

Complex and aesthetically beautiful arches may be built due to the precision engineering involved in the fitting of voussoirs.

3. Geometry's Undisputed Victory:

The Romans used geometric principles to ensure precision, symmetry, and equilibrium in their building and engineering projects.

Aesthetically beautiful Roman buildings, such temples and basilicas, were constructed using the design principles of symmetry and proportion.

The dome of the Pantheon was designed to be perfectly spherical, and this shape was obtained through precise geometric calculations.

The Long-Term Effects

1. The New Renaissance. During the Renaissance period, classical styles and forms were revived after European builders rediscovering and adopting the classical principles of Roman building.

Andrea Palladio, a Renaissance architect, created what is known as Palladian architecture, which borrowed substantially from Roman styles like the use of columns and pediments.

The neoclassical movement, which flourished in the 18th and 19th centuries, was largely responsible for the imposing public structures we see today.

2. Cutting-Edge Technology: The Romans left a significant impact on modern engineering, especially in concrete technology and structural design.

The invention of reinforced concrete in the 19th century brought Roman concrete techniques into the modern era of building.
- Suspension Bridges The design of current suspension bridges was influenced by Roman bridge-building skills.

UNESCO World Heritage Sites   The historical and cultural significance of many Roman architectural and technical marvels has been preserved thanks to their designation as UNESCO World Heritage Sites.   Organisations and governments worldwide are still spending money to protect and restore ancient Roman architecture.

In conclusion, Roman engineering and architecture stand as an enduring symbol of humanity's inventiveness, creativity, and relentless pursuit of perfection. Some of the world's most recognisable and long-lasting buildings date back to ancient Rome, when architects and engineers were able to blend practicality with aesthetics. Their work has influenced generations of architects and engineers to this day, carrying on the ancient civilization's heritage of grandeur and invention in the built environment.

6.3. Influence on Western civilization and modern governance

The Roman Legacy and Its Impact on Western Civilization and Contemporary Government

More than a millennium after its fall, the Roman Republic and Empire continue to influence Western culture and politics. The political, legal, and cultural conditions of today's world are largely the product of Roman ideals, institutions, and contributions. In this analysis, we dive into the ways in which Roman rule has left an indelible impression on contemporary governance and political theory.

The Roman Republic, Part I: The First True Democracy

Republican Principles No. 1:

The Roman Republic, which began in 509 BC and lasted until 476 AD, was a revolutionary experiment in government that formed the cornerstones of modern democracy.

The Romans held a strong belief in the need of citizens being involved in the running of their government.

Elected officials were tasked with serving the public interest and maintaining law and order.

Repubican Government:

Citizens of the Roman Republic elected representatives to represent their interests in government.

The Roman Republic's policy and legislation were shaped by two separate but equally important bodies: the popular assemblies and the powerful Senate.

Modern democracies owe a great deal to the concept of electing representatives to make decisions on behalf of the people.

The Roman Legal System as a Model for Fairness

There are twelve tables:

The Twelve Tables, written down in 450 BC, laid the groundwork for the legal system of the Roman Republic.

The Twelve Tables emphasised legal equality, making sure that everyone was protected by the same rules.

Protection of property rights, contracts, and civil procedure are only a few of the ideas that paved the way for today's sophisticated legal frameworks.

Second, the Justinian Laws:

The Justinian Code was the culmination of substantial changes to Roman law that occurred during the Roman Empire.

The Justinian Code was a seminal legal book that had an impact on legal systems across Europe since it codified preexisting Roman rules.

- Stability in the Law: Modern legal systems still rely heavily on the original idea of codifying and standardising laws.

Governance by Design: Roman Institutions

One, the doctrine of the separation of powers:

In both the Roman Republic and the later Roman Empire, several branches of government had specific responsibilities.

In order to keep a check on one another's power, the consuls, the Senate, and the different popular assemblies all worked together.

Checks and balances, a cornerstone of contemporary democracies, have their roots in Roman administration.

Bureaucracy in Ancient Rome:

A highly developed bureaucracy, in charge of administration and revenue collecting, existed throughout the Roman Empire.

Roman administrative structures aided in the effective management of a massive empire.

The concept of a professional civil service is still at the heart of today's government institutions, ensuring administrative continuity.

Roman Contributions to Western Culture

Literature and language first:

The influence of Latin, the language of the Romans, may be seen in Western literature and language today.

Words and phrases with Latin roots are still commonly used in the fields of law, science, and religion.
- Literature and the Classics: The works of Virgil, Cicero, and Livy, among others, are still widely read and regarded as some of the finest examples of Western literature.

Engineering and Construction:

Arches, vaults, and massive buildings from ancient Rome are only a few examples of how the Romans revolutionised building techniques forever.

Numerous Western buildings, especially administrative centres and houses of worship, have borrowed features from Roman architecture, such as columns and domes.

Roman engineering achievements such as aqueducts and roadways have inspired contemporary infrastructure designs.

Third, Civic Participation and Citizenship:

Western conceptions of citizenship and civic engagement can be traced back to the Roman emphasis on civic duty and active participation in public affairs.

The concept that each person has both rights and obligations within their community is still fundamental to democracies.
Modern government relies heavily on civic education to foster responsible citizens.

V. Contemporary Government: The Roman Legacy

1. Government by the People:

Democracy, the rule of law, and the preservation of individual rights are the bedrock of contemporary government, and all three have their origins in Roman tradition.

Many contemporary nations have adopted constitutions that lay the groundwork for democratic government, with the latter often evoking Roman concepts of government and legal norms.

The idea of "popular sovereignty," in which authority is vested in the people and wielded by their duly chosen representatives, is reminiscent of classical Roman republicanism.

Law and Order:

Modern legal systems are heavily influenced by Roman legal doctrines, especially the concepts of codifying laws and guaranteeing equal protection under the law.

Many nations in Europe and elsewhere adhere to the civil law tradition, which has its origins in Roman legal ideas.

The international legal system owes a great deal to the ancient Roman practise of codifying laws and developing legal concepts.

3 Public Utilities:

Modern methods of public works and urban planning can trace their roots to Roman inventions in infrastructure like roads, bridges, and aqueducts.

Transportation in the Modern World: Roman road-building techniques and philosophies have often served as inspiration for contemporary transportation networks and engineering projects.

The Romans laid the groundwork for modern urban planning practises, such as water and sewage systems.

Conclusion: Leaving a Lasting Impact

Roman culture has left an indelible mark on Western culture and contemporary administration. Everything from the foundations of modern democracies and legal systems to the architectural marvels that never cease to amaze, the Roman Empire left an indelible mark on the world. The influence that Rome's political, cultural, and judicial systems have had over the centuries is proof of the timeless quality of some ideas and institutions. The heritage of Rome is not merely a relic; it is an active force that has shaped and is shaping our modern world.

Chapter 7:
" Important People in Roman History "

7.1. Julius Caesar: Rise and fall

The Triumph and Decline of the Roman Hero Julius Caesar

One of history's most recognisable individuals, Julius Caesar had both a dizzying rise to power and a terrible fall from grace throughout his life and career. The trajectory of Western culture was significantly influenced by his life and accomplishments as well as the intricate political and social milieu of ancient Rome. In this investigation, we look into Julius Caesar's incredible journey, analysing his rise to power, his achievements for Rome, and the causes of his fall from grace.

I. Childhood and Early Years

One, Patrician ancestry from birth:

On July 12 or 13, 100 BC, Gaius Julius Caesar was born into the aristocratic Roman family of the patrician class. His ancestors said they were descended from the Trojan prince Aeneas.

Goals from the Start:

Caesar's interest in politics and leadership was evident even at a young age. To prepare himself for his future vocation, he took courses in rhetoric, philosophy, and law.

3 Climb the Cursus Honorum Ladder:

Caesar was able to rise through the ranks of the Roman government thanks to the formalised path of political offices known as the cursus honorum. Before becoming praetor in 62 BC, he served as quaestor and aedile.

Popularity and Military Victory in Part Two

Battles fought in Gaul by the Roman army

From 58 to 50 BC, Caesar led military campaigns in Gaul, or modern-day France, which helped establish his reputation and power. With the spoils of his triumphs, he amassed money and a devoted army.

Caesar's operations in Gaul expanded Roman territory and delivered significant wealth to the city.

Commentarii de Bello Gallico, or "Commentaries on the Gallic War," are written reports of these campaigns that contributed to his growing notoriety.

2 The Public's Approval Rating:

Caesar's military achievements and populist tactics endeared him to the average Romans and won him their support.

To win over the populace, he used the age-old strategy of "Bread and Circuses," in which he subsidised grain prices for the poor and funded lavish public spectacles.

A direct threat to the Senate's authority was posed by Caesar's rising power.

The First Triumvirate and the Establishment of a Governing Structure

One, the First Triumvirate:

The First Triumvirate was a political partnership created by Caesar, Pompey the Great, and Crassus in 60 BC. Caesar's standing in Roman politics was bolstered thanks to this arrangement.

The Triumvirate was able to keep the Senate at bay by striking a delicate balance between the various interests of its members.

Caesar got himself appointed consul in 59 BC and had Pompey and Crassus named governors of the provinces under his control.

2. The Victory of France:

Caesar came to Rome in 49 BC to celebrate a splendid triumph after his campaigns in Gaul. Many senators were alienated by his displays of riches and power.

The Tipping Point and the Beginning of the Civil War

The Rubicon, Number One:

The Senate had ordered Caesar to disband his army and return to Rome as a private citizen in 49 BC, which presented a serious problem for the dictator. Caesar notoriously defied the Senate's commands and crossed the Rubicon River, setting off a civil war.

Caesar's remarks as he crossed the Rubicon have come to represent finality: "Alea iacta est" (Latin for "the die is cast").

Second, Pompey's Civil War Defeat:

In a series of engagements, Caesar's troops faced up against those of Pompey and the Senate. The Roman Civil War, as it was often known, occurred between the years 49 and 45 BC.
- Pharsalus: Pompey was defeated and forced to flee to Egypt, where he was later killed, after the decisive Battle of Pharsalus in 48 BC.

Caesar's victory and subsequent return to Rome as the city's only ruler, with the official title of "dictator perpetuo," represents a consolidation of power.

Reforms and Dictatorship in the Time of Julius Caesar

First, the Policies and Changes:

Caesar, throughout his reign as dictator, instituted a number of reforms designed to improve the state of the Roman economy, society, and government.

Land redistribution: Caesar's land reforms helped the urban poor and veterans alike get access to land.

The Gregorian calendar we use today is based on Julius Caesar's introduction of the Julian calendar.

Caesar's policy of granting citizenship to residents of conquered territory helped to further the Roman Empire's goal of unifying its many disparate parts through a common culture.

2. Obstacles and Rivalry:

Caesar was met with hostility and anger despite his many successes, especially from some members of the Roman Senate who viewed his ascendancy as a threat to the republican system.

Concerns over Caesar's rise in status as a result of his collection of honorifics, such as "dictator for life," was voiced by several senators.

Conspiracies against Caesar were fostered by claims that he had monarchial ambitions.

The Ides of March, Part VI: Assassination and Consequences

One, the Plot Against Caesar:

Brutus and Cassius were among the Roman senators who planned to kill Caesar. They executed their plot in a horrific assassination in the Senate chamber on March 15, 44 BC, often known as the Ides of March.

The conspirators justified their actions by claiming they were protecting the Roman Republic from oppression.

Immediate Consequences:

The murder of Caesar caused political upheaval in Rome. The Republic was not restored by his death; rather, it became more unstable.

- The Rise of Octavian: After Caesar's death, his adopted son and heir, Octavian (after known as Augustus), became a major player in the struggle for control of the Roman Empire.

VII. The Aftermath of Julius Caesar

1. The Fall of the Roman Empire:

The death of Caesar was a watershed point in Roman history. As the Roman Empire took over, the Roman Republic effectively ended.

2. Implications for Contemporary Politics:

Many plays, novels, and nonfiction works have explored the rise and fall of Caesar. His name is now commonly associated with authoritarian rule and political aspirations.

William Shakespeare's "Julius Caesar" is an excellent play that delves deeply into ideas of political power, treason, and conspiracy.

History of Law and the Calendar:

Caesar's influence lives on in areas beyond politics, including as law and chronology.

The Julian calendar, which Caesar introduced, served as the basis for the Gregorian calendar that is used today.

Reforms and codification of laws: his work paved the way for future judicial systems.

To sum up, Julius Caesar's life and career are a fascinating demonstration of the nuances of authority, ambition, and the changing nature of the Roman Republic. His assassination and the following growth of Rome into an empire after he had risen to power via military might and political alliances are etched in stone. Insights on the complexities of leadership, governance, and the human quest for power can be found in the study and contemplation of Julius Caesar's legacy.

7.2. Augustus: Founding the empire

The Roman Empire owes much to Augustus, its architect.

Augustus, or Gaius Octavius Thurinus as he was more often known, is widely regarded as one of the most pivotal figures in history. The political, social, and cultural environment of the ancient Mediterranean was profoundly altered throughout his rule, which marked the transition from the Roman Republic to the Roman Empire. Augustus, the man who established the Roman Empire and paved the way for its imperial dominance for centuries, is the subject of this investigation.

I. Origins and Political Career

First, the House of Octavian:

On September 23, 63 BC, Augustus was born to a family with extensive political connections. He was the adopted son and great-nephew of the famous Roman leader Julius Caesar.

Second, Julius Caesar's ruthless murder:

Brutus and Cassius were among the senators who plotted and carried out the assassination of Julius Caesar in 44 BC. Caesar named Octavian as his heir in his testament, catapulting the young man into the centre of Roman politics.

In the Third Triumvirate,

After Caesar's death, Octavian formed the Second Triumvirate with Marcus Antonius (Mark Antony) and Marcus Aemilius Lepidus in 43 BC. The goal of this political coalition was to avenge Caesar and restore order in the Roman Republic.

In order to consolidate their rule, the Triumvirs instituted proscriptions, a string of harsh purges against political opponents.

Assaults from Antony and Cleopatra, Part 2

Partition of Lands:

Octavian and Mark Antony worked along at first, but later on, problems arose between them. Their animosity was worsened by the division of regions and struggles for dominance.

Octavian in the West: Octavian established his authority over the provinces to the west, which included Italy and Gaul.

When Antony sided with Cleopatra, queen of Egypt, he was accused of treason and decadence. - Antony and Cleopatra in the East.

2. The Actium Conflict:

The Battle of Actium, fought in 31 BC, was the final confrontation between Octavian and Antony. Under Agrippa's leadership, Octavian's navy crushed Antony and Cleopatra's army, ultimately ending their ambition for power.

Augustus' Third Reign

1. Augustus's Rise to Power: Octavian returned to Rome after his triumph at Actium and immediately set about strengthening his grip on the throne. He realised he had to portray himself as a republican hero rather than a monarch.

Octavian rechristened himself "Augustus" in 27 B.C., taking on a more dignified and authoritative sounding moniker than his birth name, Otacianus, but stopping short of formally seizing the throne.

Augustus instituted a new type of governance called the principate, in which he exercised absolute power while giving the impression of retaining the Republican institutions of the past.

Governance and Policy Changes

Augustus instituted reforms and programmes designed to strengthen and secure the Roman Empire.

- The Deeds of the Divine Augustus are chronicled in Augustus' "Res Gestae Divi Augusti" ("Deeds of the Divine Augustus").

Construction of roads, bridges, and aqueducts were only a few of the many public works projects that Augustus began throughout his reign.

The Pax Romana, a period of peace and stability that lasted for around two centuries, is sometimes linked to his rule.

Augustus and the Roman Army in World War IV

One, the Legions have become more professional.

The professionalisation and rigorous training of the Roman legions began under Augustus' watch.

He widened the boundaries of the Roman Empire and fortified it with defensive frontiers like the Rhine and the Danube.

- Loyalty to the Emperor: The legions swore allegiance directly to the emperor, solidifying his authority over the armed forces.

The Military Successes of Augustus   During his reign, Augustus was successful on the battlefield, and his conquest of Egypt in 30 BC meant the end of the Ptolemaic dynasty.

onsolidating Roman rule over the Iberian Peninsula, Augustus finished the annexation of Hispania (modern-day Spain and Portugal).

He widened Rome's sphere of influence in the Balkans by adding new territory, such as Illyricum (present-day Croatia, Slovenia, and Bosnia), to the Roman Empire.

Reforms in the Arts and Religion

1. Restoring Old Morals and Values

Augustus aimed to revive long-lost Roman norms like family values, decency, and religious devotion.

He passed moral legislation, including statutes that promote marriage and procreation and prohibitions on gluttony and adultery.

The Second Great Awakening:

Augustus played a significant role in religious affairs and is sometimes credited with revitalising traditional Roman religion.

His position as Rome's high priest, or Pontifex Maximus, gave him oversight of the religion of the state.

Augustus sanctioned the creation of an imperial religion in which his deified image was worshipped long after his death.

Augustus's Lasting Impact, Part VI

Roman Empire, No. 1: During Augustus's rule, the Roman Republic formally became the Roman Empire. His principate served as a template for later imperial administration.

When Augustus adopted Tiberius as his heir, he established a precedent for the peaceful transition of power.

Tiberius, Caligula, Claudius, and Nero were all members of the Julio-Claudian dynasty, which he established during his reign.

Funding for the Arts:

Augustus was a supporter of the arts, and throughout his rule, Roman culture and literature flourished.

- Literary Accomplishments: He lived during the flourishing of the works of such great poets as Virgil, Horace, and Ovid.

The Ara Pacis, the Mausoleum of Augustus, and the restoration of the Temple of Apollo on the Palatine Hill were just a few of the architectural marvels that Augustus oversaw throughout his reign.

Third, Impact on Upcoming Leaders:

Successive Roman emperors followed Augustus' lead in a number of ways, including adopting imperial titles like "Augustus" and "Princeps. The principate system instituted by Augustus served as a model for the administration of the Roman Empire for centuries.

VII. Concluding Thoughts: A Lasting Mark
We owe much of what we know about government, leadership, and the development of history to Augustus, the first Roman emperor. The lasting impact of the Roman Empire on Western civilisation may be traced back to his political acumen in the tumultuous latter years of the Roman Republic, his military successes, and his cultural and religious reforms. Augustus represents the power of one person to alter the course of history and make an everlasting impact on the world via their leadership, and his legacy lives on as a symbol of transition and creativity.

7.3. Constantine the Great: Conversion to Christianity and the Byzantine Empire

The Christianization of Constantine the Great and the Establishment of the Byzantine Empire.

A turning point in human history can be found in the life and rule of Constantine the Great, also known as Constantine I. His political and military successes, as well as his decision to become a Christian, had far-reaching effects on the Roman Empire and its successor, the Byzantine. Constantine the Great's life is investigated in detail, including his decision to become a Christian, the signing of the Edict of Milan, and the subsequent foundation of the Byzantine Empire as a successor to the Roman one.

I. Origins and Political Career

1. Origins and Family History:

   On February 27, 272 AD, in what is now Ni, Serbia, Constantine the Great was born. His father, Constantius Chlorus, was an officer in the Roman army, hence he was born into a prestigious family.

The Tetrarchy, Part 2:

   The Tetrarchy, a form of government with four emperors including Diocletian and Maximian, ruled the Roman Empire in the early fourth century AD. One of these emperors was Constantius Chlorus, who ruled under the name Augustus.

Third, Constantine's Ascendancy:
   Politics and war both played a role in Constantine's rise to power. When Constantine's father died in 306 AD, his warriors in the western provinces declared him Augustus.

Constantine fought a number of wars and disputes with other factions who wanted to be emperor.

II. Becoming a Christian

1) A glimpse of the future at the Milvian Bridge battle:

The purported vision that Constantine had just before the Battle of Milvian Bridge in 312 AD was one of the defining moments of his life. Legend has it that Constantine looked up to the sky and saw the chi-rho () symbol with the words "In this sign, conquer."

When Constantine realised that his vision was a message from God, he made the decision to become a Christian.

The Chi-Rho became an important Christian emblem by combining the first two Greek characters for "Christ" (O and X).

Second, the Milanese Edict (313 A.D.)

The Edict of Milan was issued by Constantine and Licinius, the eastern Augustus, in 313. The persecution of Christians ended with the promulgation of this edict, which gave religious freedom across the Roman Empire.

The Edict of Milan was a watershed milestone in the history of religious freedom, signalling the end of state-sanctioned persecution.

Constantine's Religious Change of Heart

With his conversion to Christianity, Constantine broke with the longstanding practise of Roman emperors adhering to the polytheistic beliefs of ancient Rome.
Shortly before his death on May 22, 337 AD, Constantine had himself baptised.

Part Three: The Rise of the Byzantine Empire

Establishment of Constantinople

The establishment of Constantinople as the new capital city in 330 A.D. is one of Constantine's most enduring legacies. Constantinople (today's Istanbul, Turkey) was the capital of the Byzantine Empire for more than a thousand years due to its strategic location at the crossroads of Europe and Asia.

Natural defences and access to important trade routes were both made possible by Constantinople's position on the Bosphorus Strait.

Constantine considered himself to be the legitimate emperor of the Roman Empire, and he named his capital city Constantinople, or "New Rome."

Restructuring the Bureaucracy

During Constantine's rule, the Roman Empire underwent a number of administrative reforms designed to bolster its might.

He split the Roman Empire in two, making Constantinople the capital of the eastern half and Rome the seat of power in the west.

Constantine minted a new gold coin called the solidus, which quickly gained widespread acceptance and became a stable part of the economy.

Third, a concentration of authority:

By doing so, Constantine hoped to strengthen his grip on power inside the empire and advance Christianity.

- The First Council of Nicaea, a meeting of Christian bishops called by Constantine in 325 AD to settle theological issues, especially the Arian controversy.

Constantine's endorsement of Christianity increased the Church's prestige inside the Roman Empire and marked the beginning of the Church's institutionalisation.

Part Four: The Empire of Constantine the Great

Roman and Byzantine Heritage 1

The empires of Rome and Constantinople were irrevocably altered by his rule.

He was instrumental in the process of converting the Roman Empire to Christianity, paving the way for its later triumph in the Byzantine Empire.

The Byzantine legal system was profoundly impacted by Constantine's administrative and legal changes.

- Imperial power: Constantine's legacy gave rise to the idea of a strong centralised power in the Byzantine Empire.

Diversity and Acceptance of Religions 2:

Byzantine society was able to accommodate a wide range of faiths thanks to Constantine's promotion of religious tolerance and the Edict of Milan.

The Byzantine Empire was home to people practising a wide range of faiths, from Christianity and Judaism to paganism.

The Christian Church in the Byzantine Empire struggled with theological discussions and the creation of orthodox doctrines, hence the terms "Orthodoxy and Heterodoxy."

3. Importance in the Arts and Architecture

The Hagia Sophia and the Hippodrome are just two of the many architectural achievements that followed Constantine's decision to establish the city of Constantinople.

Mosaics, icons, and ornate building plans are all hallmarks of the distinctive artistic style that emerged under the Byzantine Empire.

Fourth, the Roman Empire underwent a metamorphosis:

The Roman Empire underwent a dramatic transformation during Constantine's reign. His acceptance of Christianity and the subsequent foundation of Constantinople as the eastern capital established the framework for the unique character and longevity of the Byzantine Empire.

The Emperor Who Formed an Empire, Part V

An everlasting impression on history was made by Constantine the Great's adoption of Christianity and his reforms to the Roman Empire's political and religious institutions. The Byzantine Empire, a continuation of the Roman legacy, began during his rule and lasted for nearly a millennium. The fact that Constantine converted to Christianity, instituted administrative reforms, and laid the groundwork for what would become Constantinople attests to his status as a transformative character in Roman and Byzantine history.

Chapter 8:
"The Roman Way of Life"

8.1. Roman society and classes

What the Roman Social Classes Reveal About Ancient Life

Ancient Roman society was highly stratified and hierarchical, and it had a significant impact on the development of human civilization. There were clearly defined social classes in Roman society, from the earliest days of the Roman Republic to the height of the Roman Empire. In this investigation, we delve into the complex web that was Roman society, looking closely at the numerous social strata that made it up and the mechanisms that dictated their interactions with one another.

I. The Ancient Roman Social Order

Patristic Rulers, No. 1:

The patricians of ancient Rome made up the uppermost social stratum of the empire. They were the elite, having come from long-established Roman families. The political authority and influence of the Patrician class was substantial.
- Positions of political power: patricians held most of the highest offices in the Roman Senate throughout the early Roman Republic.

They had the ability to own land, go to school, and have a say in political matters, among other privileges.

The Plebeians, Second:

The vast majority of Romans were considered to be plebeians. They were the regular folks, including farmers and shopkeepers and factory workers. When they weren't given a voice in politics at first, they demanded it.

Plebeians fought for equal rights and representation in the Roman government through various political campaigns, such as the Conflict of the Orders.

Diversity of Economic Status: Plebeians included a wide spectrum of socioeconomic classes, from poor workers to prosperous merchants.

Slavery in Roman Culture Part II

Persons Held in Slavery:
Roman society depended heavily on its slave population. Slaves, who the Romans gained through invasion or desperation, helped out in many spheres of daily life and the economy.

Slaves were also used as domestic servants, performing jobs including cooking, cleaning, and caring for children.

Many slaves were used for agricultural labour on latifundia, or enormous agricultural estates.

Influence on the Economy:

Slavery was vital to the Roman economy because it provided a ready supply of inexpensive labour.

Slavery exacerbated economic inequalities in Roman society because it allowed wealthy landowners to profit from the work of enslaved people.

Rights of Roman Citizens, Part III
Legal status as a citizen:

Citizenship under the Roman Republic was much sought after because of the many benefits that came with it, including the ability to vote and hold public office. However, not every Roman citizen had the right to vote in imperial elections.

The aristocratic and plebeian classes constituted the bulk of Roman citizens. Citizenship was often awarded to family members or as a prize for bravery.

While foreigners (known as peregrini) were allowed to live in Roman territory, they were barred from voting and holding public office.

Legal Protections:

Legal safeguards and the guarantee of a fair trial were provided to Roman citizens. Roman law served as the basis for the judicial system, and all trials took place in open court.

Byzantine Emperor Justinian's codification of Roman law left an indelible mark on international law.

Part Women's Involvement

Roles of Men and Women

Gender roles in Roman society were strictly defined. Women were expected to stay at home and take care of their families.
Domus: A woman's major role in Roman society was as the head of the household (domus) and primary caretaker of her children.

Women had few protections under the law and were not allowed to vote or run for public office.

Famous Ladies:

Even though most Roman women did not hold public office, many did. Livia, Augustus's wife, and Agrippina the Younger, who wielded considerable political power, are two such examples.

Women of the imperial dynasty, such as empresses and princesses, frequently played significant roles in imperial politics and administration.

IX. The Roman Empire

Family patriarch

The patriarch of a Roman family was called the paterfamilias. He held a lot of sway over his household members, including his wife, kids, and slaves.

The paterfamilias had the right to make decisions for his family's welfare under the law.
He also had an important part in the family's religious events and observances.

The Family Unit:

The Roman family was large and typically included several generations all living under the same roof. It served as the cornerstone of Roman society.

Roman households valued blood ties and made sure to keep things in the family for as long as possible.

Having offspring and continuing the family name was highly valued, therefore marriage was seen as an important institution.

The Roman Forum as a Hub of Public Activity

1. Centralised Government and Business: In ancient Rome, the Roman Forum was the nerve centre of the city's civic, political, and economic activities. Important government buildings were located there, and it also served as a lively marketplace and venue for public speeches and gatherings.

The Roman Senate, an important political body, held its sessions in the Curia Julia, a structure close to the Forum.

Citizens and officials alike would convene at the Forum for public debates, speeches, and discussions on political issues.

2. Shrines and Memorials:

The Forum was filled with memorials to deities, emperors, and military triumphs.

As a symbol of Rome's wealth and power, the treasure was stored in the Temple of Saturn.

The destruction of the Second Temple and the fall of Jerusalem in 70 A.D. are commemorated by the Arch of Titus.

VII. Alteration in Social Status

The Potential for Advancement in One's Social Status

Although there was a clear social hierarchy in Roman culture, there was still room for advancement. People and their families could rise to prominence through successful military service, the accumulation of money, or political achievements.

The equestrians were a prosperous middle class that comprised merchants, business owners, and even some officers in the armed forces.

People who had been enslaved but were afterwards manumitted were able to become Roman citizens and fully participate in Roman culture.

The Dynamics Are Changing

Conquest, immigration, and economic shifts all played a role in shaping the changing dynamics of Roman society over time.

The expansion of Roman cities provided people with new options for finding work and interacting with their neighbours.

The Roman Empire's extensive boundaries allowed for the spread of ideas and customs from all over the known world.

Final Thoughts on a Complex Society

Roman culture was complex and ever-changing, with its own set of norms on gender roles, marriage, and the law. It was crucial in shaping Western civilisation and its legacies in fields like law, government, and architecture live on today. Roman civilization, like a tapestry, is a complex reflection of ancient existence, revealing the depth and diversity of human experience and altering the path of history for millennia to come.

8.2. Family life and religion

Ancient Roman Society's Foundational Elements

Every aspect of ancient Roman society, from its social structure and everyday rituals to its politics and government, could be traced back to the importance of family life and religion. Roman society was organised around the nuclear family, or "familia" in Latin, and religious practises pervaded all facets of daily life. This investigation delves into the complex relationship between family and religion in ancient Rome, illuminating the norms, practises, and beliefs that shaped Roman culture.

A. The Roman Social System

Family patriarch

The patriarch, or paterfamilias, was the most powerful member of a Roman family. The male leader of the household, known as the paterfamilias, had complete control over his household members, including his free and enslaved family members.

The patriarch of the family had the final say on matters of life and death, as well as major family matters like marriage and inheritance.

As the family priest, he was an integral part of the family's religious ceremonies and rituals.

2. The Family with Multiple Generations:

Many Roman households consisted of several generations who all shared the same home. The emphasis on blood ties and close relatives was bolstered by this set-up.
Family ties were strong since many generations of relatives lived under one roof.

When you think of a Roman home, what comes to mind is the "domus," the place where you and your family eat, sleep, and go about your daily business.

Part Two: Women's Place at Home

Roles of Men and Women

In ancient Roman culture, women were expected to focus solely on domestic duties. The patriarch of the family was the ultimate arbiter of these responsibilities.

The wife and mother, or "domina," was responsible for running the household and supervising activities including cooking, cleaning, and taking care of children.

Women had few protections under the law and were not allowed to vote or run for public office. Some women from aristocratic families, however, held significant power in the background.

Second, Parenthood and Marriage:

Roman society relied heavily on marriage, and bearing offspring was highly prized so that the family name could continue. Women in Roman society were expected to get into marriage and to have children.

Mothers were held in high regard and given the title "matronae." They were primarily responsible for fostering the development of morally upright offspring.

Marriages in ancient Rome were typically arranged by the bride's family, as the idea of marrying for love was uncommon at the time.

Religious Practises in Ancient Rome

The Roman Pantheon and the Origins of Polytheism

The Romans held a polytheistic worldview, worshipping a pantheon of deities who represented different parts of life, nature, and civilization. Jupiter, Juno, Neptune, and Venus were only few of the gods that made up the Roman pantheon.

Every Roman home featured a shrine, called a "lararium," devoted to the lares and penates, guardian deities of family and property.

Roman religion encompassed governmental rituals and ceremonies to the gods in addition to private ones held inside families.

Two Types of Religious Practises:

The Romans practised their religion both in public and in private. The ludi (games) and religious processions were two examples of state-sponsored public celebrations. The patriarch was responsible for leading private family rituals of worship.

Members of the household offered prayers, incense, and food to their deities on a daily basis as part of private rituals.

Romans celebrated many holidays all year long, including Saturnalia and a holiday honouring the god Janus.

Syncretism between religions and foreign cults

First, a blending of faiths:

The Romans were tolerant of the introduction of new gods and philosophies, which resulted in religious syncretism. By doing so, they were able to incorporate the deities of the peoples they subjugated into their own religion.

For instance, the Asia Minor goddess Cybele was later incorporated into Roman religion.

Second, Secret Faiths:

The Roman Empire saw a rise in the popularity of mystery religions, which are characterised by hidden rituals and initiation processes. These cults made bold claims of bringing about one's complete and total metamorphosis.

For instance, people from many walks of life participated in the mystery cults of Mithras, Isis, and the Eleusinian Mysteries.

Ancestral Reverence and Funeral Rites

Funerary Customs

Roman funeral customs had strong theological underpinnings. It was important to the Romans, who believed in an afterlife, for their deceased to have a dignified passage into the next world, thus they held elaborate funeral ceremonies.

Cremation was the most frequent practise for getting rid of bodies after death. Ashes were kept in urns and buried in family plots after cremation.

Through ceremonies and offerings, families kept a close connection to their ancestors even after they had passed away.

Honouring One's Dead:

The Roman religion and household culture heavily emphasised honouring one's ancestors. Ancestral spirits, or "manes," were thought to watch over and guide the living.

The Parentalia was a celebration held in memory of ancestors who had passed away. Families would pay their respects to the dead by visiting cemeteries, bringing presents, and sharing meals.

Conclusion: The Roman Cultural Groundwork

The Roman family and the Roman religion were the bedrocks of ancient Roman society, providing the foundation for the values, rituals, and beliefs that came to characterise Roman culture. A key institution in upholding social order and passing on cultural norms was the family, with its hierarchical structure and intergenerational families. The Romans' religion was intricately woven into their daily lives, and it included both private and public rites to help them feel closer to the divine.

Roman family life and religion had a significant impact on the growth of Western civilisation, and this is their ongoing legacy. The lasting impact of Roman culture can be seen in the ways in which contemporary societies are influenced by Roman ideas like the nuclear family, ancestor worship, and religious syncretism.

8.3. Entertainment, including gladiatorial games and theater

From the Gladiator Games to the Theatre: Ancient Roman Entertainment

The ancient Romans relied heavily on entertainment as a means of escape, stimulation, and cultural expression. From the gory displays of the gladiatorial games to the cerebral and artistic pursuits of the theatre, Roman culture flourished on a diverse tapestry of amusement. This study delves into the varied realm of ancient Roman amusement to give light on the many sorts of Roman leisure time pursuits.

I. The Gladiator Games and the Colosseum

First, the Colosseum:

The Flavian Amphitheatre, or the Colosseum, is an iconic representation of Roman entertainment. This massive stadium, finished in 80 AD, could hold more than 50,000 people.

Architectural Wonder: The Colosseum's smart layout and crowd management systems made it possible to host a wide variety of events.

The Colosseum was principally used for gladiatorial combat, in which trained warriors fought to the death in elaborate and often melodramatic fights.

2 Gladiators:

Slaves or prisoners of war were trained to fight professionally as gladiators. They competed in the arena for the amusement of the audience after receiving training in various forms of fighting.

The heavily armoured retiarius and the net-wielding secutor were only two examples of the many gladiator specialisations.

- Schools and Barracks: Gladiators formed tight-knit communities through their training and living arrangements.

Three, the Games

The gladiatorial games were highly organised affairs with officials, sponsors, and a strict schedule for each bout.

These events drew huge audiences because of their popularity. Exotic animals and naval battles staged inside the Colosseum boosted the overall showmanship.

The games were utilised as a political tool by the emperors to spread their message and win over the public.

Theatrical and Performing Arts Section II

1. Ancient Roman Drama:

In ancient Rome, the theatre was a popular source of entertainment. The Romans incorporated aspects of comedy and tragedy from Greek drama into their own unique kind of theatre.

Romans of all socioeconomic backgrounds regularly attended performances of humorous and serious plays at open-air theatres.

Plautus and Terence, two of the most famous Roman playwrights, wrote comedies that drew on commonplace situations and humour.

Amphitheatres and Live Shows: Roman cities frequently included amphitheatres built specifically for theatrical events. The theatres had sophisticated stage designs and excellent acoustics, and they could seat vast crowds.

The Romans were big fans of mime and pantomime, forms of performance art that use a mix of mime, dance, and music to communicate a message.

Roman theatre relied heavily on music and choral performances to evoke a range of emotions from the audience.

Third, the Circus Maximus and the Sport of Chariot Racing

The Greatest Circus Ever:

The main event in the massive Circus Maximus was chariot racing. It is centrally located in Rome and has a capacity of 250,000 spectators.

Chariot races, with expert charioteers vying for fame, were the most well-known spectacles at the Circus Maximus.

In the ancient sport of chariot racing, competitors were divided into groups known as "factions," with each group identified by a different colour.

The Four Essential Elements:

The Blues, Greens, Reds, and Whites were the four prominent teams in chariot racing. Allegiance to one's faction was deeply embedded in Roman identity, and each of these groups attracted devoted followers.

Charioteers and spectators alike took great pride in their allegiance to one of the many competing factions, and it was not uncommon for competition between them to break out onto the streets of Rome.

Charioteers had the potential to amass fame, fortune, and social standing.

4th: Spas and Recreational Activities

First, the ancient Roman baths:

Thermae, the Roman term for public baths, served as hubs for more than just personal hygiene in ancient Rome.

Roman baths were elaborate architectural complexes that included swimming pools, saunas, and both hot and cold baths.

- A Gathering Place: Baths were places where people might get together for conversation, physical activity, and rest. There was also philosophical and intellectual discourse during these gatherings.

2: Recreational Pursuits

The Romans enjoyed a wide variety of pastimes, including gambling, board games, and dice games.

The Romans had their own version of chess and checkers called Ludus Latrunculorum, which was played on a square board with pieces depicting Roman troops.

Playing dice games like "tesserae" was a popular pastime for individuals of all socioeconomic backgrounds.

V. Recreation and Dining

First, Feasts and Banquets:

In ancient Rome, dining was a popular kind of entertainment, particularly among the upper class. Banquets, also known as "convivia," were lavish events including delicious food, wine, and lively entertainment.

The banquets were hosted in special rooms called "triclinia," where the guests sat on couches and were served by slaves.

Music, dance, and recitations of poetry were common forms of entertainment during banquets.

2. Symposiums:

Food, drink, and stimulating conversation all came together during symposia. Conversations and deep musings on life's big questions might be had during these gatherings.

Notable philosophers such as Cicero and Seneca participated in philosophical conversations at symposia. Topics of discussion included ethics, politics, and literature.

VI. Concluding: An Enchanting Web of Fun

Roman entertainment reflected the ideals, preferences, and social structures of the time and included a wide range of activities. Romans looked for entertainment, thrills, and chances to relax and socialise in a variety of forms, from the huge spectacles of the Colosseum to the intellectual pursuits of the theatre. These entertainments not only enthralled the Roman public, but also influenced Roman society and created a legacy that still has an impact on today's shows and games.

Chapter 9:
" Roman Military Technology "

9.1. The Roman legions and their tactics

Masters of Ancient Warfare: Roman Legions and Their Strategies

In the annals of military history, the Roman legions hold a place of honour as a paragon of military discipline, organisation, and tactical prowess. These elite armies were crucial to the success of the Roman Republic and Empire, helping the Romans expand their territory and maintain control over it. In this investigation, we travel to the ancient world of the Roman legions and learn about the organisation, education, weaponry, and strategy that made them the undisputed leaders of battle.

I. Legion Organisation in Ancient Rome

1. Generations and Elders:

   The cohort was the lowest level of organisation in a Roman legion's chain of command. Each legion had about 5,000 men in its ranks, divided into ten cohorts.

   The legion's leadership was built on the shoulders of the centurions. A centurion was in charge of each cohort and was responsible for keeping order and leading the troops into combat.

   - Centuries: Each century was made up of a group of cohorts and led by a centurion. The centuries were the smallest tactical units of the legion, with only 80-100 men.

Infantry Legion:Infantrymen made up the bulk of the legion and were called "legionaries." These men, all Roman citizens, had rigorous military training and strict discipline.

Legionaries wore segmented armour called lorica segmentata, carried rectangular shields called scutums, wielded short swords called gladii, and threw javelins called pilums.

Drills, weapon practise, and formation drills were all staples of the Roman legionaries' training regimen.

Forces auxiliary:

Auxiliary forces, generally comprised of non-citizens, were commonly included in Roman legions alongside legionaries. These auxiliary soldiers were used as cavalry, archers, and skirmishers, among other roles.

Auxiliaries were specialised units that served as an integral part of the legions by providing support, versatility, and specialised skills and tactics.

Instruction and Discipline for the Roman Legion

1: Forming and Drilling

The Roman Legion had rigorous training in drill and formation. One of the hallmarks of Roman discipline was the army's ability to preserve unity under fire.

To defend themselves from incoming projectiles, Legionaries would march in a disciplined formation called the "testudo" (tortoise).

Romans used a variety of combat formations, such as the "triplex acies," a battle line with three divisions, and the "wedge" formation, which was used to burst through enemy lines.
Combat drills: Roman soldiers were given intensive instruction in swordplay, shield technique, and close quarters warfare.
Legionnaires typically carried the gladius, a short stabbing blade.

Legionnaires were adept at hurling pilum, a type of javelin, to disperse opposing formations before closing in for close quarters combat.

Roman shields, such as the scutum, were employed both as a defensive tool and an offensive weapon, therefore Roman troops learned techniques like shield pounding and shield pushing.

Obligation and Discipline 3.

The Roman army was famous for its strict discipline. Legionnaires pledged their devotion to their commander and the Roman state by taking an oath of service.

Flogging, forced labour, and even execution were all used as tools of discipline by Roman commanders.

- Legionary Pride: The Roman legion was the foundation of the Roman soldier's strong esprit de corps.

Equipment for the Roman Legion III.

1. The Segmented Lorica:

The lorica segmentata was a very recognisable piece of Roman legionary gear. Metal plates that locked into each other offered both protection and mobility.

The lorica segmentata was more comfortable to wear and provided superior protection for its wearers compared to prior forms of armour.

The segmented armour used by Roman legionaries is a defining feature of their legendary appearance.

Gladius 2: For Roman legions, the gladius was the basic issue sword. It was a little sword made for quick thrusts and slashes.

The gladius proved particularly useful in the close quarters fighting that characterised so many Roman conflicts.

Legionnaires' backup weapon was a dagger called a pugio, which they carried alongside their gladius.

Throat (Scutum):

The scutum was a wooden shield with layers of linen and leather covering its rectangular shape. It was an essential feature of Roman defence strategy and offered superior protection.

Overlapping shields provided a strong shield wall, or "testudo," for legionaries to use against incoming bullets.

The scutum wasn't merely a defensive weapon; it could also be used offensively to bash foes and knock them off their feet.

Tactics of the Roman Legions, Part IV

The Testudo Group, No. 1: Roman legionaries used the testudo, or tortoise formation, as a defensive strategy against missile strikes, such as those from archers and slingers.

In this formation, soldiers would form an almost impenetrable shell by firmly interlocking their shields above and to the sides.

Although the testudo provided outstanding defence, it was too cumbersome to move around in during a siege or a rocket attack.

2: Attacking Tactics The Roman army used a wide variety of offensive strategies. The pilum was used to confuse opponent formations, the wedge formation was used to break through enemy lines, and the "testudo" was used to advance while under fire.

When everything else failed, Roman commanders would resort to "decimation," a practise whereby one out of every ten recalcitrant troops in a unit would be executed by their fellow soldiers.

Battles at a Siege:

The Roman legions were experts in siege warfare, and they used siege engines and strategies to take control of heavily fortified cities and strongholds.

Battering rams, siege towers, and ballistae were only some of the siege machines that Roman engineers created.

Roman trench warfare consisted of encircling and isolating enemy strongholds through the use of trenches, fortifications, and protective earthworks.

Masters of Ancient Combat, Finale
The Roman legions were symbols of the empire's discipline, organisation, and strategic brilliance, not only its superb troops. Roman legionaries were feared on the battlefield thanks to their distinctive armour and weapons, extensive training, and flexible tactics. Because of their skill, Rome was able to establish and maintain the largest empire in human history, forever altering the development of military strategy.

The legions of Rome left an indelible mark on the evolution of warfare and are still influential today. Military strategy and leadership still draw heavily on the legions' guiding ideals of discipline, training, and tactical inventiveness.

9.2. Famous Roman military campaigns

The History of Notable Roman Military Operations and Their Impact

Famous military campaigns that left an indelible effect on the globe may be found throughout the history of ancient Rome. Roman legions fought a series of epic battles from the early days of the Roman Republic to the height of the Roman Empire, which resulted in the expansion of the empire's borders and a significant impact on the development of the world. Here we examine the tactics, decisive battles, and lasting legacies of many famous Roman military campaigns.

During the Punic Wars, I.

One, the Punic War (264–241 BC)

Rome and Carthage, two major Mediterranean powers, fought for many years in the First Punic War. The island of Sicily served as the primary battleground.

During the war, Rome bolstered its navy to challenge Carthage's dominance at sea. The corvus, a gadget used for boarding, was a game-changer when it was first introduced.

Treaty of Lutatius: Rome took control of Sicily and Carthage gave up land in exchange for peace and an end to hostilities in 241 BC.

In the Second Punic War (218-201 BC),

Perhaps the most well-known of the Punic Wars is the Second Punic War, also known as the Hannibalic War. It was about the daring invasion of Italy by the renowned Carthaginian general Hannibal Barca.

For example, in 216 BC, during the Battle of Cannae, Hannibal famously led his army through the Alps and on to victory over the Romans.

By defeating Hannibal in the Battle of Zama in 202 BC, Roman general Scipio Africanus changed the course of the war and helped bring about a peace deal in 201 BC.

There was a third Punic war (149-146 BC).

The ultimate confrontation between Rome and Carthage occurred during the Third Punic War. The Roman devastation of Carthage epitomised this period.

- The Roman siege of Carthage lasted three years and ended in the city's destruction in 146 BC.

The Roman Empire grew larger and more powerful when it won the Third Punic War and established its control over the Mediterranean.

The Gallic Wars of Julius Caesar (58-50 BC)

The military battles led by Roman general and future ruler Julius Caesar against numerous Gallic tribes are known as his "campaigns in Gaul."

Caesar's consolidation of power and the enormous wealth and prestige it brought to Rome are both attributable to his conquest of Gaul.

Caesar's first-hand descriptions of the Gallic Wars, referred to as the "Commentarii," are a rich source of information about Roman military strategy and tactics.

The Roman Civil Wars, Part III

First, the Civil War of Sulla (88-87 BC)

For control of the Roman Republic, Lucius Cornelius Sulla and Gaius Marius fought a bitter civil war.

- Proscriptions: Proscriptions were a hallmark of Sulla's leadership, in which those seen to be enemies of the state had their property seized and were sometimes put to death.

Victorious and assuming the mantle of dictator, Sulla was the first Roman to do so in over a century.

The Second Civil War of Caesar (49-45 BC)

Wars sprang out between supporters of Julius Caesar and those of the Roman Senate, led by Pompey the Great.

Caesar's crossing of the Rubicon River in 49 BC sparked the civil war and inspired his now-famous statement, "Alea iacta est" (Latin for "The die is cast").

The Battle of Pharsalus, fought in 48 B.C., marked the beginning of Caesar's rise to power in Rome.

The Fourth Battle of Actium (c. 30 B.C.):

The decisive conflict between Octavian (later Augustus) and the united ships of Mark Antony and Cleopatra occurred at the battle of Actium in 31 BC.

Augustus' victory at Actium marked the official end of the Roman Republic and the birth of the Roman Empire.

After the war, Augustus moved quickly to secure his dominance over Egypt, ensuring a steady supply of grain and riches for the expanding empire.

Five, the Dacian Wars of Trajan (AD 101-106)

Impressive engineering marvels and a successful invasion defined Emperor Trajan's battles against the Dacian realm, which was located in what is now Romania.

The Roman soldiers were able to cross the Danube River and invade Dacia because of the bridge that Trajan's engineers built over the river.

A victory monument, Trajan's Column, depicting the campaigns, and the acquisition of Dacia as a Roman province culminated from the Dacian Wars.

Conflicts with the Parthian Empire (52 B.C.–217 A.D.)

The Roman Empire and the Parthian Empire were at war for several centuries. During that time, important wars took place, such as the doomed invasion led by Roman general Crassus in 53 BC and the Parthian expedition led by Emperor Trajan in 114 AD.

The hit-and-run tactics of Parthian mounted archers posed a significant threat to Roman troops.

Extensive territory was acquired in the East as a result of Trajan's Parthian expedition, which included the conquest of Armenia.

Seventh Century A.D. (AD 69), the Year of the Four Emperors:
After the death of Nero, the year known as "The Year of the Four Emperors" was distinguished by a string of civil conflicts and fast leadership transitions.

This turbulent year saw four different emperors—Galba, Otho, Vitellius, and Vespasian—lay claim to the throne.

- The Triumph of Vespasian: Vespasian won, establishing the Flavian dynasty and bringing peace and stability to Rome.

Marcomannic Wars, VIII (AD 166–180):

The Roman Empire's northern frontier was the site of the Marcomannic Wars, a series of campaigns fought against Germanic and Sarmatian tribes.

Emperor Marcus Aurelius led the Roman army into battle against the invading barbarians, and he encountered severe difficulties.

The campaigns demonstrated the need for a resolute defensive posture along the borders of the empire.

Consequences and History

The transformation of the Roman state from a republic into an empire was mirrored in the breadth and duration of the legendary Roman military operations. The political landscape and the growth of Western civilisation were both moulded by the Roman military's campaigns.

These campaigns left an indelible mark on history through the expansion of the Roman Empire, the introduction of Roman law and government to newly conquered lands, and the maturation of Roman military tactics and strategy. The lasting significance of Rome's military triumphs on the global arena is highlighted by the fact that lessons learnt from these operations continue to inform military thought and strategy to this day.

9.3. Decline of the Roman military

The Weakening of the Roman Army: The Loss of Influence and Strength

There are several factors that contributed to the demise of the Roman military, but ultimately their efforts helped bring down the Western Roman Empire. The Roman legions, once the unrivalled military might of the ancient world, saw their power and capacities gradually erode over the course of several decades. We examine the many causes of the Roman military's collapse, from internal problems like corruption and difficulties in recruiting to external dangers like barbarian invasions.

Internal Aspects, Part I

First, political instability and corruption:

Corruption among the Roman military and government grew as the empire expanded. Military discipline and effectiveness suffered as emperors and provincial governors took advantage of their positions for personal gain.

A rise in the use of mercenaries and other non-citizen soldiers in the Roman military weakened the previous legions' famed devotion and unity.

Frequent civil wars within the empire added to the burden on the armed forces. Because of internal strife and pressure to take sides, several legions were unable to effectively protect the empire.

Problems with the Economy:

Inflation that was out of control and a lack of available resources were just two of the problems facing the Roman economy. The military's capacity to pay for personnel and supplies was severely hampered by the current economic climate.

Inadequate pay and supplies were a common source of discontent and low morale among the armed forces.

The purchasing power of military salaries was diminished due to the debasement of silver and gold coins in Roman money.

Third, Challenges in Recruiting:

It grew harder and harder to keep up a permanent army force through recruitment and upkeep. Due to the economic burdens and dangers involved with military service, fewer citizens were eager to serve.

The Roman army's reliance on mercenaries and recruits who weren't Roman citizens damaged the army's sense of national pride even as it met short-term manpower needs.
Recruits had less experience and discipline because the quality of recruits had decreased over time.

Dangers from Without

1. Invasion by Savages:

The Visigoths, Vandals, Huns, and Ostrogoths, among others, constantly invaded the Roman Empire. The military's ability to protect the expansive borders was tested by these intrusions.

The Visigothic sack of Rome in the year 410 AD was a stunning event that demonstrated Rome's weakness.
Midway through the fifth century, the Hunnic invasion led by Attila the Hun threatened the heart of the empire, and only diplomacy and money prevented calamity.

Overexertion, secondly:

The vastness of the Roman Empire made it harder to administer and defend. The sheer size of the empire put a strain on the armed forces and made it difficult to successfully counter challenges on several fronts.

The Roman Empire's partition into the Eastern and Western halves drained its resources and diverted attention from foreign defence to internal strife.

Lack of Enough Soldiers It grew harder and harder to muster enough legions to protect far-flung regions.

Military Restructuring:

Military reform efforts frequently failed or were wrong. When it came to the military, many emperors tried to make administrative adjustments in an attempt to solve the difficulties that plagued the force.

By expanding the size of the army and creating new organisational structures, Emperor Diocletian sought to bolster the might of the Roman Empire. Although these procedures were partially effective, they did not resolve the underlying problems within the armed forces.

Although a more professionalised army had resulted from the Marian reforms of the late Republic, the system had eventually become entangled in corruption and factionalism.

Adaptations to New Societies and Cultures

First, a Values Shift:
There was a shift in Roman society away from an emphasis on martial virtues and citizenship. Serving in the military was no longer

looked upon as a noble way to gain Roman citizenship or social standing.

There was a decline in enlistments due, in part, to the popularity of pacifist ideas.

With more people living in cities, fewer people from rural areas were available to join the Roman army.

Second, the decline of military customs:

The legions' declining relevance and replacement by other military groups represented the deterioration of Roman military traditions and discipline.

The non-Roman allies known as foederati and the movable field troops known as comitatenses both rose to prominence in the later Roman military.

Less effective Romanization of these non-citizen warriors led to less unified and disciplined fighting units.

Western Roman Empire's Collapse, Part IV
The Deposition of Odoacer (476 A.D.)
Romulus Augustulus's ouster as emperor of the Western Roman Empire in 476 A.D. by the Germanic chieftain Odoacer marked the final stage in the decline of the Roman military.

Although this was the final stage of the Western Roman Empire's protracted fall, it is commonly seen as the symbolic end of the empire.

The Eastern Roman Empire, often known as the Byzantine Empire, maintained its military and administrative structure for several more centuries, proving that the Eastern Roman legacy was resilient.

The Roman Army's Lasting Impact:

Despite the collapse of the Western Roman Empire, the Roman military's influence lived on in many forms. Roman military strategy, organisation, and engineering advancements left an everlasting imprint on later civilizations and military traditions.

There were several internal and external forces that contributed to the downfall of the Roman military. Once the most powerful army in antiquity, the Roman legions gradually weakened due to factors like corruption, economic issues, recruitment difficulties, external threats, and shifting societal ideals, ultimately leading to the collapse of the Western Roman Empire. Although the Roman Empire eventually fell, the lasting influence of Roman military accomplishments may be seen in the ways in which military theory and strategy have evolved throughout the centuries since Rome's fall.

Chapter 10:
Historical Analysis and Contexts "

10.1. Ancient and modern interpretations of the rise and fall

The Fall of the Roman Empire: Ancient and Contemporary Theories

The rise and fall of the Roman Empire, one of history's most recognisable and consequential civilizations, has long fascinated students of history and thinkers from all walks of life. The rise and fall of Rome has been interpreted in numerous ways, both in antiquity and the modern era. In this investigation, we examine the major narratives and ideas that have arisen over the centuries regarding the development and fall of the Roman Empire from both ancient and modern viewpoints.

I. Definitions from Antiquity

To begin with, Livy's Platonic History:

In his massive work "Ab Urbe Condita" (From the Founding of the City), the Roman historian Titus Livius, better known as Livy, chronicled Roman history from its legendary beginnings through his own time.

Livy wrote his history to teach his contemporaries and posterity a lesson in morality. He believed that religion, order, and loyalty were essential to Rome's success.

Traditional Roman ideals such as frugality, courage, and civic responsibility were idealised in Livy's depiction of early Rome.

Polybius's anacyclosis theory, second:

Polybius, a Greek historian who lived during Rome's ascendance, provided a more methodical account of the city's political development in his work "Histories."

A cycle of political systems in which monarchy, aristocracy, and democracy replace one another was hypothesised by Polybius in his thesis of anacyclosis.

Polybius regarded the Roman Republic as a model of successful government because it included the best features of monarchy, aristocracy, and democracy.

Second, Contemporary Meanings

1. Gibbon's publication "The History of the Decline and Fall of the Roman Empire" :

In the 18th century, Edward Gibbon penned a classic, "The History of the Decline and Fall of the Roman Empire," which is still used as a reference today.

Gibbon's essay, titled "Decline and Fall," attempted to dissect the myriad causes of Rome's downfall. He pointed to deterioration in morality, corruption in government, and a weakening economy as major factors.

- Enlightenment Viewpoint: Gibbon, writing from an Enlightenment viewpoint, placed less emphasis on religious and supernatural causes for Rome's decline.

2. Economic and Marxist Perspectives:

Economic theories of Rome's collapse, centred on class struggles and structural difficulties, were advanced in the 20th century by Marxist historians like Rostovtzeff and Finley.

The economic factors that these researchers focused on were slave labour, exploitation, and wealth disparity.

According to the Dependency Theory, which is a modern view of Roman decline, the empire collapsed because it relied too heavily on resources from conquered lands without developing a self-sufficient economy.

Climate and the environment:

Recent research has investigated the role of climate and the environment on Rome's decline.

Some scholars have hypothesised that climate change, including cooling periods and droughts, reduced agricultural output and exacerbated political unrest.

The spread of deadly diseases like the Antonine and Cyprian plagues may have depleted the Roman military and left the country exposed to attack.

Fourth, a look at potential causes:

Many modern historians use a multicausal perspective, accepting the idea that internal and external pressures both had a role in Rome's decline.

Political instability, military difficulties, and succession problems are all said to have contributed to Rome's collapse.

New insights into the history of the Roman Empire have come from the study of other disciplines, including archaeology, environmental science, and genetics.

Interpretational Themes

1. Decline in Morality:

The moral degradation of the Roman population is commonly cited as a major cause of the city's demise in both ancient and modern accounts. Decadence, corruption, and the abandonment of traditional values are highlighted by this viewpoint.

Moral decline was a common subject in ancient accounts of Rome's decline, including those written by Livy and other ancient historians.

The contemporary perspective recognises that Gibbon's writing and many later interpretations maintained an emphasis on ethical and moral considerations.

2. Military and Political Difficulties:

A common thread in theories about Rome's demise is the part played by political upheaval and external military threats.

Polybius and Livy, two ancient authors, spoke on the difficulties of ruling a country and facing armed threats.

In modern interpretations, the effects of invasions from without, civil strife within, and the decline of Roman military might have been examined.

Third, Socioeconomic Aspects:

Modern explanations of Rome's decline place more emphasis on economic and social reasons, reflecting shifting academic attitudes.

Many Marxist historians attribute the fall of Rome to internal class strife and economic problems.

Modern studies have highlighted the possible effects of environmental changes and sickness on Roman civilization, thus it's important to consider these environmental factors.

4. Contemporary Importance

Contemporary arguments about the rise and fall of nations and empires are still influenced by the narratives of Rome's rise and collapse. The lessons learned from Rome's past are relevant to contemporary issues and policy discussions, whether they focus on the need for moral leadership, the effects of economic inequality, or the difficulty of sustaining a strong military.

The many factors that contributed to Rome's collapse highlight the difficulty of tracing their origins. As the development and fall of the Roman Empire demonstrates, there is rarely a single cause for the downfall of a great civilisation, but rather a confluence of several forces, both internal and external. Studying Rome's past is still a great way to learn about the intricacies of human cultures and the lessons they can teach us now.

10.2. Notable historians and their views

Historical Figures and Their Theories on the Decline of the Roman Empire

Historians' interest in the decline and demise of the Roman Empire spans several decades. Famous historians have commented on, analysed, and interpreted this amazing tale of the past for centuries. In this investigation, we look at how different historians have interpreted the development and collapse of the Roman Empire, illuminating the wide variety of viewpoints that have contributed to our current knowledge of this seminal time in human history.

Firstly, Edward Gibbon:

The English historian Edward Gibbon (18th century) is among the most well-known and important writers on the demise of the Roman Empire. Between 1776 and 1788, he wrote his magnum opus, "The History of the Decline and Fall of the Roman Empire," and it is still considered a classic in the field of Roman history.

Opinions of Gibbon:

First, Gibbon blamed moral degradation and corruption in Roman society for the empire's fall. His view was that the once-virtuous Roman people had become increasingly immoral and corrupt.

Second, religious considerations: Gibbon gave less weight to religious factors in the decline of Rome than he did to rational and secular ones. Christianity, he said, was not the primary reason of Rome's decline, despite being a substantial cultural upheaval.

Thirdly, political corruption was a major factor, which Gibbon emphasised, as was the incompetence and corruption of Roman leaders. He explained how many rulers cared more about their own advancement or maintaining their position in power than they did about doing their jobs as rulers.

Gibbon's study also took into account economic variables, such as soaring inflation and currency devaluation. It was his contention that Rome's economy had reached an unsustainable level.

Gibbon examined the weakening of Roman military might and discipline over time in his fifth thesis, titled "Military Decline." He blamed the erosion of ancient Roman martial values and the recruitment of non-Roman mercenaries.

Polybius, Part II:

Hellenistic historian Polybius was a Greek who witnessed the birth of Rome. His "Histories" provides an interesting modern take on Rome's rise to power from 264 BC to 146 BC.

In Polybius' Opinion:

Anacyclosis, a cyclical theory of political evolution, was first proposed by Polybius. The hybrid constitution of Rome, he thought, was the best of all possible worlds since it combined elements of monarchy, aristocracy, and democracy.

Polybius thought the Roman political system was an ideal combination of monarchy (represented by the consulship), aristocracy (represented by the Senate), and democracy (represented by the popular assemblies). He thought Rome's success may be attributed in part to the way the city was governed.

Third, Rome's military might was praised by Polybius, who believed the Roman army to be more effective than those of any other nation. Training, self-control, and flexibility were all things he stressed.

Third, Livius (or Titus) of Rome:

Augustan-era Roman historian Livy's magnum opus "Ab Urbe Condita" (From the Founding of the City) spans from the city's fabled beginnings to Livy's own time.

What Livy Thinks:

First and foremost, Livy intended for his history to serve as a source of moral instruction for his contemporaries and posterity. Piety, self-control, and patriotism were among the values he highlighted.

Livy idealised ancient Rome, painting it as a place where people lived by and upheld traditional Roman ideals of thrift, bravery, and civic responsibility. He thought that these traits were important in Rome's success.

A.J. Toynbee, 4th:

Arnold J. Toynbee, a British historian of the 20th century, is famous for his in-depth look at the rise and fall of civilizations in his book "A Study of History."

Opinions of Toynbee:Toynbee's theory of "challenge and response" formed the basis of his investigation into the decline of the Roman Empire. He maintained that the ability to adapt to changing circumstances is crucial to the survival of civilizations.

Toynbee theorised that Rome fell into decline because the city couldn't adjust to changing conditions both at home and abroad. Loss of civic morality, internal strife, and the inability to fully incorporate conquered peoples were all issues he brought up.

Toynbee argued that the Roman Empire was an example of a "universal state," and he analysed the growth and decline of other empires in his larger study of human history. Multidisciplinary Research and Contemporary Historians: Archaeology, environmental science, and genetics are just few of the many disciplines that modern historians draw from in their examination of Rome's development and fall.

Some contemporary historians investigate the impact of weather fluctuations and epidemics on the development of the Roman Empire. Others stress the social dynamics and cultural developments that shaped the empire's fate, while Marxist historians have focused on class battles and economic difficulties as crucial to Rome's decline.

Third, historians who take a multicausal perspective acknowledge that multiple forces, both internal and foreign, contributed to Rome's decline.

Interdisciplinary studies have led to a more complete picture of the development of the Roman Empire. The economic, social, and environmental conditions of ancient Rome have all been illuminated by archaeological findings.

Conclusion: Multiple Viewpoints on a Complicated Narrative

The decline and fall of the Roman Empire has long fascinated historians and been the focus of academic study. The various points of view that have informed our knowledge of this seminal time in history range from the moral and secular interpretation of Edward Gibbon to the contemporary study of Polybius and the "challenge and response" framework of Arnold J. Toynbee.

Modern historians expand upon these works, using methods and theories from a variety of fields to decode the mysterious rise and fall of the Roman Empire. Historians have worked tirelessly to further our understanding of the development and collapse of the Roman Empire by shedding new light on this fascinating period in human history.

10.3. Debates and controversies in Roman history

Roman Historical Controversies and Debates: Untangling a Tangled Web

Because of its length and complexity, the study of Roman history has occupied scholars for many years. Discussions, disputes, and divergent interpretations among historians and scholars have been generated by countless historical events, characters, and cultural changes from the early days of the Roman Republic through the fall of the Western Roman Empire. This investigation delves deep into some of Roman history's most heated arguments and conflicts, illuminating the nuances that have fascinated and perplexed scholars for centuries.

Part One: The Collapse of the Roman Empire

First, Gracchi's Revisions:

Tiberius and Gaius Gracchi instituted changes in the second century BC, although their effectiveness is still debated today. Tiberius tried to redistribute public land to reduce land inequality, whereas Gaius prioritised structural changes to society at large. Historians are split on whether or not their reforms were motivated by altruism or only a cynical ploy to seize power.

Julius Caesar's Crucial Part:

Central to discussions of Roman history are the ascent of Julius Caesar and the fall of the Roman Republic. Did Caesar's lust for power and ambition cause the downfall of the Republic, or were there other, more systemic causes? The tension between private drive and systemic flaws in the Republic remains a topic of study for historians.

The Optimates vs. the Populares, Part 3

A fundamental conflict in the politics of the late Republic is that between the senatorial aristocracy (the Optimates) and the populist reformers (the Populares). Class struggle and friction between these groups are disputed factors in the collapse of the Republic.

Part Two: How Roman Imperialism Worked

Expansionism in Rome

For ages, scholars have speculated on the reasons underlying Rome's territorial growth. Others see it as an ideological mission to expand Roman culture and rule, while still others point to the desire for wealth and security as the driving force. The morality of Roman imperialism and its effects on conquered territories are discussed.

2. Roman Peace:

Peace and stability throughout the Roman Empire's later years are celebrated and debated as the Pax Romana. Others stress the repressive aspects of Roman rule and the hardships endured by marginalised communities, while some historians claim that the Pax Romana brought wealth and cultural exchange.

Economy and Society in Ancient Rome

First, Roman Slavery's Impact on the Economy

Slavery's impact on the Roman economy is still up for discussion. Some historians stress the importance of slavery to the Roman economy, while others claim that it wasn't as crucial as previously believed. Conditions of slave labour and their relative contribution to economic output are other points of contention.

Getting Up in the World

Social mobility in ancient Rome is a hotly debated topic. Historians disagree on whether or not people could climb the social ladder and whether or not class and ethnicity were obstacles.

Culture and Religion in Roman Society

One, the conversion of the Roman Empire to Christianity:

Christianity's rapid expansion throughout the Roman Empire is hotly contested. Its rapid expansion and eventual replacement of traditional Roman religious practises are subjects of historical investigation, as are the roles played by Constantine the Great and other influential figures.

Multiculturalism and the Roman Sense of Self:

There is some disagreement on what it means to be Roman and how multicultural Rome actually was. Researchers look at how local identities developed and developed within the context of the empire's religious and cultural diversity.

War and Defence

Achieving Military Victory in Rome:

Exactly how the Roman military managed to build and keep up such a massive empire is a topic of conjecture. The success of Roman military strategy, organisation, and discipline are studied, along with the roles played by various military leaders.

Two Reasons for the Fall of the Roman Army:
Researchers look closely at how the Roman military's deterioration contributed to the collapse of the Western Roman Empire. Challenges

in recruitment, economic stresses, and external dangers are all issues that historians have speculated on as undermining military efficiency.

The Collapse of Western Roman Rule, Part VI

Comparing Economic Decline to Outside Threats

A lot of people have different ideas on what happened to bring down the Western Roman Empire. While some historians place more emphasis on external challenges like barbarian invasions, others point to internal issues like economic collapse, corruption, and inefficient administration.

2. Importance and Timing:

The fall of the Western Roman Empire and the reasons behind it are also the subject of heated historical discussion. How did things fall apart, quickly or slowly? While many believe the fall to have had far-reaching effects, others see it more as a turning point than a final catastrophe.

VII. Original Documents and Scholarly Analysis

1. The Trustworthiness of Ancient Documents:

Ancient texts, such as those written by Roman historians like Livy and Tacitus, have a long history of controversy around their veracity. Questions of bias, accuracy, and the limitations of the remaining records provide difficulties for historians.

Second, Alternative Theories:

Historians who hold revisionist ideas present competing narratives of Roman history and give critical analysis. As a result of these viewpoints, long-held assumptions are frequently questioned, and fresh discussions are sparked.

Relevance in the Present Day

Roman history's many disputes and conflicts teach us much about the intricacies of human politics, culture, and society. They promote analytical pondering on such topics as the relative importance of persons and institutions in moulding our understanding of the past and the value of considering alternative points of view while constructing our own historical narratives.

Additionally, modern debates on issues like government, imperialism, social dynamics, and the rise and fall of civilizations all have parallels and lessons to learn from the study of Roman history. Historians add to our knowledge of the Roman world by participating in these discussions, and they also contribute to broader discussions about the intricacies of human history and its lasting importance.

www.ingramcontent.com/pod-product-compliance
Lightning Source LLC
LaVergne TN
LVHW010222070526
838199LV00062B/4683